Passwords
Social Studies Vocabulary
Medieval to Early Modern Times

CURRICULUM ASSOCIATES®, INC.

To the Student

What is **chivalry**? Where is **Mesoamerica**? How is a **theory** different from a **hypothesis**? *Passwords: Social Studies Vocabulary* will help you learn the words you need to do well in social studies. The lessons in this book are about social studies topics you will be studying.

Every lesson focuses on ten words that will help you understand the topic. The lessons include a reading selection that uses all ten vocabulary words. Four practice activities follow the reading selection. Using each vocabulary word many times will help you remember the word and its meaning. A writing activity ends the lesson. You will use the vocabulary words you have learned to write a journal entry, a letter, a narrative, or a description.

If you need help with a vocabulary word as you do the activities, use the Glossary at the back of the book. The Glossary defines each word and shows you the correct way to pronounce the word. It also has pictures to help you understand the meaning of difficult words.

As you work on the lessons, you may learn other social studies words besides the vocabulary words. Keep track of those other words in My Social Studies Vocabulary on pages 94–98.

Turn to pages 99 and 100 to learn about roots, prefixes, and suffixes. Find out how they can help you understand social studies words.

ISBN 978-0-7609-4497-4
©2008—Curriculum Associates, Inc.
North Billerica, MA 01862
No part of this book may be reproduced by any means
without written permission from the publisher.
All Rights Reserved. Printed in USA.
15 14 13 12 11 10 9 8 7 6 5 4 3 2 1

Table of Contents

empire   territory   decline   tax   conquer
emperor   capital   corrupt   barter   senate

What makes an empire strong and powerful? What causes a powerful empire to become weak? Read this selection to find out some of the reasons for the fall of the Roman Empire.

The Fall of the Roman Empire

A Powerful Empire

The Roman Empire was powerful for hundreds of years. An **empire** is a large area of land ruled by one person. The male ruler of an empire is called an **emperor**. At the height of its power, the Roman Empire controlled a large area of land around the Mediterranean Sea. This **territory** was about the size of the United States. The city of Rome was the capital. A **capital** is the center of a country's government. A series of good emperors had made the empire strong. They had fair laws. They treated people well. They made the empire rich through trade.

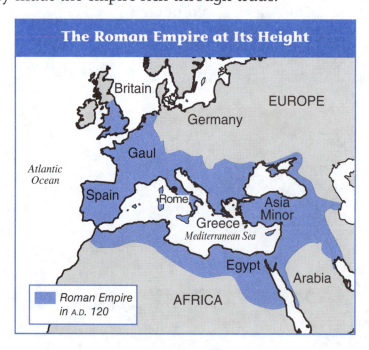

The Roman Empire at Its Height

Britain

EUROPE

Germany

Gaul

Atlantic
Ocean

Spain   Rome   Asia
                         Minor

Greece
Mediterranean Sea

Egypt

Arabia

Roman Empire
in A.D. 120

AFRICA

A Weak Empire

In A.D. 180 the Roman Empire began to **decline**, or grow weak. There were many reasons why the empire began to lose its power. New emperors were poor leaders. Some of them were cruel and did not care about the people. Others were **corrupt**, or dishonest.

Many people stopped trusting the government. Wealthy citizens stopped paying taxes. A **tax** is money people pay to support the government. Wages fell. Money began to lose its value. This caused prices to go up. People stopped using money issued by the emperor. They began to **barter**, or trade goods without using money. People were poor and hungry. Fewer people went to school. More people became slaves. Disease spread through the empire. Soon, law and order broke down.

Roman coins often showed a likeness of the emperor.

The Fall of Rome

Tribes attacked the empire from the east and the west. Finally, the empire split in two. It was divided into the Western Roman Empire and the Eastern Roman Empire. However, Rome continued to decline. In A.D. 476, invaders were able to **conquer,** or defeat, Rome.

Lasting Achievements

Many of our ideas about government and law came from the Romans. An important part of the Roman government was the senate. The **senate** is a body of the government that makes laws. Today, the United States and other countries in the world each have a senate.

The Romans also had many achievements in the arts. The works of great Roman writers and artists are still admired today. The Romans also had new ideas about building. Roman styles of arches and domes appear in many modern buildings.

Laws were made in the Roman senate.

My Social Studies Vocabulary

Go to page 94 to list other words you have learned about the fall of the Roman Empire.

| empire | territory | decline | tax | conquer |
| emperor | capital | corrupt | barter | senate |

A. *Fill in the blanks with the correct vocabulary word.*

1. to trade goods without using money

   — — — — — —

2. a large area of land ruled by one person

   — — — — — —

3. a body of the government that makes laws

   — — — — — —

4. to grow weak

   — — — — — — —

5. to defeat

   — — — — — — —

6. the city where the center of government is located

   — — — — — — — —

7. dishonest

   — — — — — — —

8. a large area of land

   — — — — — — — — —

9. the male ruler of an empire

   — — — — — — —

10. money people pay to support the government

    — — —

empire	territory	decline	tax	conquer
emperor	capital	corrupt	barter	senate

B. *Circle the word that makes sense in each sentence. Then write the word.*

1. Another word for *ruler* is (empire, emperor). _____

2. Washington, D.C., is an example of a (territory, capital).

    _____

3. A person may have to try many times to (conquer, corrupt) a bad habit.

    _____

4. My friend wants to (decline, barter) her bicycle for my skateboard.

    _____

5. Much of the (territory, senate) of the Roman Empire was located near the

    Mediterranean Sea. _____

6. Being part of a (barter, senate) means voting on new laws.

    _____

7. A dreadful cough revealed the (decline, tax) of her health.

    _____

8. Most cities charge a (tax, capital) for dog and cat licenses.

    _____

9. An (empire, emperor) can cover a vast area and be made up of many different

    lands and people. _____

10. We knew he was a (corrupt, conquer) judge because he took bribes.

    _____

WORD ROOT

The word **territory** comes from the Latin root
terra, which means "land" or "earth."

empire	territory	decline	tax	conquer
emperor	capital	corrupt	barter	senate

C. *Choose the correct vocabulary word to complete each sentence.*

1. Rome was the _____ of the Roman Empire.

2. After money lost its value, people started to _____ for the goods they needed.

3. At the height of the Roman Empire, the northern border of its _____ stretched all the way to Britain.

4. The leader's _____ actions destroyed his career.

5. Any increase in the amount of _____ due to be paid will bring many complaints.

6. Daily life became more difficult when a dreadful disease spread through the _____ .

7. Because of the Romans, many countries in the world today have a _____ as part of their government.

8. It was the duty of the _____ to protect and defend Roman citizens.

9. Weak leadership was one of the causes for the _____ and fall of the Roman Empire.

10. The weak state of the empire made it easier for tribes to attack and _____ Rome.

The Fall of the Roman Empire

| empire | territory | decline | tax | conquer |
| emperor | capital | corrupt | barter | senate |

D. *Use each word in a sentence that shows you understand the meaning of the word.*

1. decline _____

_____

2. capital _____

_____

3. tax _____

_____

4. emperor _____

_____

5. empire _____

_____

6. territory _____

_____

7. corrupt _____

_____

8. senate _____

_____

9. conquer _____

_____

10. barter _____

_____

Write!

Write your response to the prompt on a separate sheet of paper. Use as many vocabulary words as you can in your writing.

Imagine you are Rome's last emperor. Write a letter to the citizens of Rome about changes you will make to try to save the empire.

The Fall of the Roman Empire

9

LESSON 2

trade	foundation	reform	code	saint
merchant	adviser	scholar	mosaic	Christianity

What steps can a ruler take to build a new empire? Read this selection to find out about the Byzantine Empire and two of the emperors who helped it rise to power.

The Byzantine Empire

A New Capital and Empire

Before the fall of Rome, the Roman Empire was split in two. A Roman emperor named Constantine moved the capital, or center, of the empire to a new city in the east. The new capital was the old Greek city of Byzantium. He rebuilt the city and renamed it Constantinople. Rome and the western part of the empire fell. The eastern part grew rich and powerful.

The new capital had a good location. It lay between two seas. It also lay between Europe and Asia. As a result, Constantinople became a center of trade. **Trade**, the buying and selling of goods, made the empire and

Emperor Constantine paid to build a new capital city for the Byzantine Empire.

its merchants very wealthy. A **merchant** is someone who makes money by buying and selling goods. Emperor Constantine laid the **foundation**, or base, for the Byzantine Empire. The empire lasted for nearly 1,000 years.

Emperor Justinian

In A.D. 527, Justinian became emperor. He was a strong ruler. He took back some of the land the Roman Empire had lost. He made the Byzantine Empire larger. Justinian ruled the empire with the help of his wife, Empress Theodora. She was his trusted adviser. An **adviser** is a person who gives advice.

The Justinian Code

Justinian also wanted to **reform**, or improve, the empire's laws. He ordered scholars to make the laws easier to understand. A **scholar** is a learned person. The new code was known as the Justinian Code. A **code** is a group of laws organized in a clear way. Empress Theodora helped women in the Byzantine Empire gain some important rights, too.

Byzantine Buildings and Art

Justinian and other Byzantine emperors built hundreds of churches, palaces, and other buildings throughout the empire. The most famous church in Constantinople is the Hagia Sophia. The church still stands today. Inside the church there are many beautiful mosaics. A **mosaic** is a picture made from small pieces of colored stone or glass. Most of the mosaics show saints. A **saint** is a holy person.

The Spread of Christianity

Christianity emerged during the Roman Empire. **Christianity** is a religion based on the life and teachings of Jesus. Christianity became the main religion in the Byzantine Empire.

The laws that Emperor Justinian reformed became the Justinian Code.

Emperor Justinian built many beautiful churches, such as this one.

This mosaic shows Empress Theodora, wife and adviser of Emperor Justinian.

My Social Studies Vocabulary

Go to page 94 to list other words you have learned about the Byzantine Empire.

trade	foundation	reform	code	saint
merchant	adviser	scholar	mosaic	Christianity

A. *Match each word with its meaning. Write the letter of the correct meaning on the line in front of each word.*

1. ＿＿ adviser

2. ＿＿ saint

3. ＿＿ trade

4. ＿＿ reform

5. ＿＿ Christianity

6. ＿＿ code

7. ＿＿ merchant

8. ＿＿ mosaic

9. ＿＿ foundation

10. ＿＿ scholar

a. a picture made from small pieces of colored stone or glass

b. a group of laws organized in a clear way

c. a person who gives advice

d. a base for something

e. a learned person

f. a holy person

g. to improve

h. the buying and selling of goods

i. a person who makes money by buying and selling goods

j. the religion based on the life and teachings of Jesus

trade	foundation	reform	code	saint
merchant	adviser	scholar	mosaic	Christianity

B. *Circle the word that makes sense in each sentence. Then write the word.*

1. As the emperor's (adviser, scholar), she influenced his decisions.

   _____

2. Inside the church was a beautiful (merchant, mosaic) in gold and blue.

   _____

3. The emperor planned to (trade, reform) the laws in order to make them easy

   to understand. _____

4. The (saint, scholar) had studied law for many years.

   _____

5. An emperor made (foundation, Christianity) the official religion.

   _____

6. People could more easily understand the empire's laws because of the new

   (code, mosaic). _____

7. The figure of a (code, saint) was shown in many works of Byzantine art.

   _____

8. In his shop, the (adviser, merchant) sold spices and honey.

   _____

9. By moving the capital to Constantinople, the emperor set in place the

   (foundation, Christianity) of the Byzantine empire. _____

10. The Byzantine Empire built its wealth through (reform, trade).

   _____

WORD ROOT

The word **scholar** comes from the Latin word **schola**, meaning "school."

| trade | foundation | reform | code | saint |
| merchant | adviser | scholar | mosaic | Christianity |

C. *Choose the correct vocabulary word to complete each sentence.*

1. The judge referred to the _____ to find the exact law.

2. The woman could not decide which color of silk cloth to buy from the

   _____ .

3. The religion of _____ spread to the Byzantine Empire.

4. The growth of the city depended upon _____ with Asia.

5. People prayed in front of the picture of a _____ .

6. As the Roman Empire fell, Constantine built the _____

   of a new empire.

7. Empress Theodora became an important _____

   to her husband.

8. The _____ was highly respected for her knowledge

   of mathematics.

9. It was important to _____ the city's laws so that all citizens

   would be treated equally.

10. The artist cut the colored glass into small pieces to arrange a

    _____ .

The Byzantine Empire

trade	foundation	reform	code	saint
merchant	adviser	scholar	mosaic	Christianity

D. *Use each pair of words in a sentence.*

1. trade, merchant

_____

_____

_____

2. foundation, Christianity

_____

_____

_____

3. adviser, scholar

_____

_____

_____

4. reform, code

_____

_____

_____

5. mosaic, saint

_____

_____

_____

Write!

Write your response to the prompt on a separate sheet of paper.
Use as many vocabulary words as you can in your writing.

Imagine you are a visitor to Constantinople, the great capital of the Byzantine Empire. Write a postcard to a friend about the city and describe what daily life is like there.

What do you think it would be like to live in a desert region? How might the desert affect your way of life? Read this selection to find out about the empire that arose in the deserts of Arabia.

The Muslim Empire

A Desert Way of Life

Arabia is in Southwest Asia. Most of Arabia is a vast desert. Very little rain falls in this **arid**, or dry, region. Fresh water is found only at an oasis. An **oasis** is an area in the desert that contains underground water.

The desert affected the way early Arabs lived. Some Arabs settled near an oasis. There they farmed or raised animals. Some of these Arabs became traveling merchants. They carried goods across the desert in caravans. A **caravan** is a group of people traveling together by camel. Other Arabs became desert herders. They were nomads. A **nomad** moves from place to place. Nomads searched for food and water for their herds.

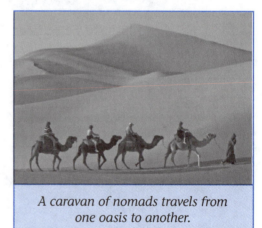

A caravan of nomads travels from one oasis to another.

The Growth of Trade and Cities

More Arabs moved to oasis villages. Soon, these villages became market towns and cities because of trade. Cities also grew along trade routes. Arabia had a good location for trade. It stood between Asia, Africa, and Europe. Many bodies of water also surrounded Arabia. Therefore, cities in Arabia became important trade centers.

Mecca became the largest and richest trading city. It also was an important center of religion. Each year, people came from all over Arabia. They were on a pilgrimage to Mecca. A **pilgrimage** is a journey to a holy place.

The Prophet Muhammad

In A.D. 570, Muhammad was born in Mecca. He became a wealthy merchant. One day, Muhammad said, an angel visited him. The angel told him, "You are the Messenger of God." Muhammad returned home and began to **preach**, or teach a religious message. Muhammad told people to worship only Allah. *Allah* is the Arabic word for "God." At that time, Arabians believed in many gods. They did not trust Muhammad's message at first.

Eventually, people began to believe Muhammad was God's prophet. A **prophet** is a person who is inspired to speak for God. Many people became followers of Muhammad. **Islam** is a religion based on the teachings of Muhammad. A **Muslim** is a person who believes in Islam.

The Spread of Islam

Muhammad died in A.D. 632. By then, Islam had spread across Arabia. After Muhammad's death, caliphs continued to spread Islam. A **caliph** is a Muslim ruler. The caliphs expanded the Muslim Empire. They spread Islam through the Middle East and into North Africa by defeating other empires. Muslim merchants also helped to spread Islam to Southeast Asia and West Africa.

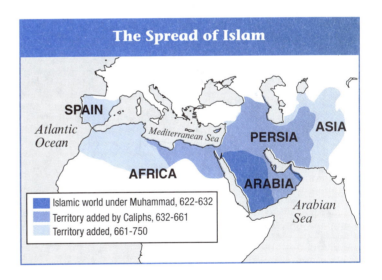

The Spread of Islam

SPAIN

Atlantic Ocean

Mediterranean Sea

AFRICA

PERSIA

ASIA

ARABIA

Arabian Sea

■ Islamic world under Muhammad, 622-632
■ Territory added by Caliphs, 632-661
■ Territory added, 661-750

My Social Studies Vocabulary

Go to page 94 to list other words you have learned about the Muslim Empire.

The Muslim Empire

| arid | caravan | pilgrimage | prophet | Muslim |
| oasis | nomad | preach | Islam | caliph |

A. *Fill in the blanks with the correct vocabulary word.*

1. a Muslim ruler

   __ __ __ __ __ __

2. a person who moves from place to place, usually in search of food and water

   __ __ __ __ __

3. the religion based on the teachings of Muhammad

   __ __ __ __ __

4. a journey to a holy place

   __ __ __ __ __ __ __ __ __ __

5. to teach a religious message

   __ __ __ __ __ __

6. an area in the desert that has underground water

   __ __ __ __ __

7. a person who believes in Islam

   __ __ __ __ __ __

8. a person who is inspired to speak for God

   __ __ __ __ __ __ __

9. very dry

   __ __ __ __

10. a group of people traveling together by camel

    __ __ __ __ __ __ __

The Muslim Empire

| arid | caravan | pilgrimage | prophet | Muslim |
| oasis | nomad | preach | Islam | caliph |

B. *Choose and write the two words that best complete each sentence.*

| prophet | nomad | caravan | oasis |

1. A _____ and his herd of goats found water at a nearby

    _____ .

| caravan | Islam | Muslim | pilgrimage |

2. Every year people make a _____ to Mecca, which is

    a sacred place in the religion of _____ .

| Islam | caliph | prophet | Muslim |

3. A _____ is a _____ ruler who led the

    empire after Muhammad's death.

| caravan | caliph | oasis | arid |

4. The hot sun beat down on the _____ land and the

    _____ of tired travelers and their camels.

| Muslim | preach | prophet | caliph |

5. Muhammad was a _____ who began to

    _____ to others about believing in only one God.

WORD ROOT

The word **prophet** comes from the Greek root **phanai**, meaning "to speak."

arid	caravan	pilgrimage	prophet	Muslim
oasis	nomad	preach	Islam	caliph

C. *Choose the correct vocabulary word to complete each sentence.*

1. The religion of _____ is based on the teachings of Muhammad.

2. Very little rain falls in the _____ lands of Arabia.

3. All of the camels in the _____ carried heavy loads.

4. Many people followed Muhammad to hear him _____ God's message.

5. Early Arabs built towns at an _____ so they could have water to drink and to grow crops.

6. Who was the first _____ to rule after Muhammad's death?

7. Every Muslim must make a _____ to Mecca at least once.

8. Muslims believe that Muhammad was the _____ of God, or *Allah*.

9. After Muhammad died, a series of _____ rulers expanded the empire.

10. The small flock of goats and sheep was very important to the _____ and his family.

| arid | caravan | pilgrimage | prophet | Muslim |
| oasis | nomad | preach | Islam | caliph |

D. *Use each word in a sentence that shows you understand the meaning of the word.*

1. caravan _____

_____

2. nomad _____

_____

3. prophet _____

_____

4. preach _____

_____

5. Islam _____

_____

6. arid _____

_____

7. Muslim _____

_____

8. oasis _____

_____

9. caliph _____

_____

10. pilgrimage _____

_____

Write!

***Write your response to the prompt on a separate sheet of paper.
Use as many vocabulary words as you can in your writing.***

Imagine you are a young nomad living with your herd of animals in the
desert of early Arabia. Write a journal entry about your way of life and what
you have heard about the teachings of Muhammad.

Buddhism   reunite   bureaucracy   rank   porcelain
dynasty   imperial   scholar-official   artisan   maritime

What do you already know about China? What words would you use to describe China? Read this selection to find out about China in the Middle Ages.

China in the Middle Ages

A Time of Chaos

In A.D. 220, China broke into civil war. It was a time of great chaos. Military leaders fought against one another for control of land. This difficult period lasted for 350 years.

During this time, many Chinese people began following Buddhism. **Buddhism** is a religion that began in India. It is based on the teachings of the Buddha. Buddhism teaches that people can escape from their suffering.

Buddhism teaches that peaceful thought can overcome suffering.

New Rulers Restore Order

In A.D. 581, a general named Wendi took power. Wendi was the first emperor of the Sui dynasty. A **dynasty** is a series of rulers from the same family. By 589, Wendi had reunited China and restored order. **Reunite** means to bring together again.

Sui dynasty emperor Wendi strolls in his gardens.

The Tang dynasty followed the Sui dynasty. The Tang dynasty began in A.D. 618. It ruled for almost 300 years. The Tang emperors had to make sure China stayed together. They set up an imperial state. **Imperial** means relating to an empire or emperor. They also set up an organized government. They created a bureaucracy. A **bureaucracy** is a system of departments that carry out the work of a government. Each department was in charge of one area, such as trade, farming, or taxes.

To work in the bureaucracy, people had to take an exam about the teachings of Confucius. Confucius was a Chinese scholar. His ideas about right and wrong had guided the Chinese people for hundreds of years. A person who passed the difficult exam became a scholar-official. A **scholar-official** was a learned person with a government job. After the Tang dynasty ended, the Song dynasty expanded the exam system. Scholar-officials became a new **rank**, or social class, of people in China.

Warriors such as these made China an imperial power.

Wealth from Land and Sea Trade

China grew wealthy from trade. New roads and canals had helped to improve trade. Chinese merchants traded silk, tea, steel, and paper, made by artisans. An **artisan** is a skilled craftsperson. The Tang dynasty was famous for its porcelain. **Porcelain** is hard, white pottery made from fine clay. To pay for goods, Chinese governments were the first to print and use paper money.

Later, during the Mongol Empire and the Ming dynasty, trade expanded. China had more contact with the outside world. Early Ming emperors built large fleets. They sent the ships on **maritime**, or sea, journeys. These voyages took Chinese explorers to India, Arabia, and East Africa.

Porcelain created by Chinese artisans was traded around the world.

My Social Studies Vocabulary

Go to page 95 to list other words you have learned about China in the Middle Ages.

China in the Middle Ages

Buddhism   reunite   bureaucracy   rank   porcelain

dynasty   imperial   scholar-official artisan   maritime

A. *Match each word with its meaning. Write the letter of the correct meaning on the line in front of each word.*

1. _____ porcelain

2. _____ dynasty

3. _____ artisan

4. _____ Buddhism

5. _____ reunite

6. _____ maritime

7. _____ scholar-official

8. _____ imperial

9. _____ rank

10. _____ bureaucracy

a. social class

b. relating to the sea

c. a system of departments that carry out the work of a government

d. a learned person with a government job

e. relating to an empire or emperor

f. a series of rulers from the same family

g. a skilled craftsperson

h. hard, white pottery made from fine clay

i. the religion that began in India and is based on the teachings of the Buddha

j. to bring together again

| Buddhism | reunite | bureaucracy | rank | porcelain |
| dynasty | imperial | scholar-official | artisan | maritime |

B. *Circle the word that makes sense in each sentence. Then write the word.*

1. In a (porcelain, bureaucracy), different departments are in charge of trade, farming, taxes, and other areas of government. _____

2. The religion of (Buddhism, bureaucracy) spread throughout China because it helped people during difficult times. _____

3. To become a (scholar-official, reunite) in the Chinese government, a person had to pass a very hard exam. _____

4. Chinese craftspeople used a fine clay to make (artisan, porcelain). _____

5. To end the fighting in China, it was important to (rank, reunite) the country. _____

6. A skilled craftsperson is an (artisan, scholar-official). _____

7. China expanded its contact with the outside world through (maritime, imperial) exploration. _____

8. A new class or (rank, dynasty) of scholar-officials grew in China during the Middle Ages. _____

9. Early emperors of the Ming (maritime, dynasty) expanded trade to Arabia and Africa. _____

10. The Tang emperors set up their (Buddhism, imperial) state to keep the country together. _____

WORD ROOT

The word **imperial** comes from the Latin word **imperium**, which means "empire."

| Buddhism | reunite | bureaucracy | rank | porcelain |
| dynasty | imperial | scholar-official | artisan | maritime |

C. *Choose the correct vocabulary word to complete each sentence.*

1. The emperor held the highest _____ in Chinese society.

2. A series of _____ journeys expanded China's trade with Asia, Arabia, and Africa.

3. People often complain about the _____ of the government.

4. In a _____ , a series of rulers come from one family.

5. The religion of _____ was founded in India.

6. The talented young _____ created beautiful plates.

7. The first emperor of the Sui dynasty did many things to _____ China after years of chaos.

8. A person had to study very hard to pass the exam to become a _____ in the Chinese government.

9. Chinese emperors set up an _____ state to keep the country together.

10. Because it is made of fine clay, _____ can break easily.

China in the Middle Ages

| Buddhism | reunite | bureaucracy | rank | porcelain |
| dynasty | imperial | scholar-official | artisan | maritime |

D. *Use each word in a sentence that shows you understand the meaning of the word.*

1. porcelain _____

_____

2. maritime _____

_____

3. Buddhism _____

_____

4. artisan _____

_____

5. dynasty _____

_____

6. rank _____

_____

7. reunite _____

_____

8. scholar-official _____

_____

9. bureaucracy _____

_____

10. imperial _____

_____

Write!

***Write your response to the prompt on a separate sheet of paper.
Use as many vocabulary words as you can in your writing.***

Imagine you are either a scholar-official or an artisan living in China
during the Middle Ages. Write a journal entry about some of the changes
you have either heard about or seen take place in your country.

geography   natural resources   crossroads   prosperous   kinship
savanna   culture   revenue   griot   clan

What do you remember about the growth of empires in other regions of the world? What made them wealthy and strong? Read this selection to find out what led to the rise of empires in West Africa.

Empires of West Africa

The Geography of West Africa

During the Middle Ages, West Africa was made up of small kingdoms. The kingdoms grew into empires because of trade. The region's **geography**, or physical features, led to the growth of trade. West Africa is made up of desert, rain forest, and savanna. A **savanna** is a grassy plain with few trees. Each of these areas is rich in certain **natural resources**, or materials found in nature. These natural resources included gold. The people of West Africa traded gold and other natural resources to gain great wealth. Traders used the Niger River to move goods across West Africa.

Few trees can grow on this dry savanna.

Trade and the Empire of Ghana

A vast desert called the Sahara separates North Africa from West Africa. The Sahara is rich in salt. Mining for salt in the Sahara began in the Middle Ages. Muslim traders from North Africa crossed the desert. They brought salt to West Africa to trade for gold. The Muslim traders also brought their religion, Islam, and the Arabic language. Their **culture**, or way or life, spread.

The kingdom of Ghana became powerful and rich. It was located at a trade crossroads. A **crossroads** is a place where roads come together. Traders who passed through Ghana had to pay a tax. The tax provided the king with **revenue,** or money. Ghana also controlled the gold supply. Cities in Ghana became **prosperous**, or rich, centers of trade. Ghana was the first empire to develop in West Africa.

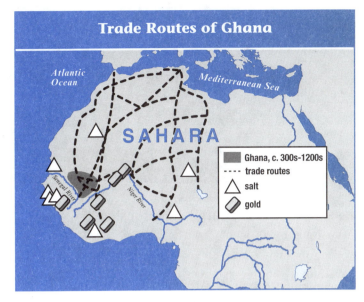

The Empire of Mali

After Ghana fell in the 1200s, the empire of Mali rose to power. It developed in the southern part of what had been the empire of Ghana. Like Ghana, Mali used trade to grow wealthy and powerful. Mali's great king was Sundiata. Stories about Sundiata have been passed down by West African griots. A **griot** is a storyteller. Sundiata was very popular. He made the gold and salt trade even more prosperous than it had been during Ghana's empire.

Art from the empire of Mali is now in museums all over the world.

West African Society

Kings ruled the powerful empires of West Africa. However, people felt a stronger tie to their families and villages. Kinship groups were the foundation of many African societies. **Kinship** is a family relationship. Kinship groups related by an ancestor formed a larger group called a **clan**. Griots passed on the history of a clan or kinship group through stories.

My Social Studies Vocabulary

Go to page 95 to list other words you have learned about the empires of West Africa.

geography   natural resources   crossroads   prosperous   kinship

savanna   culture   revenue   griot   clan

A. *Fill in the blanks with the correct vocabulary word.*

1. a family relationship

    — — — — — — —

2. a storyteller

    — — — — —

3. a grassy plain with few trees

    — — — — — — —

4. a kinship group related to a common ancestor

    — — — —

5. materials found in nature

    — — — — — — — — — — — — — — —

6. rich

    — — — — — — — — — —

7. the way of life of a group of people

    — — — — — — —

8. a place where roads come together

    — — — — — — — — — —

9. money that a government receives

    — — — — — — —

10. the physical features of a region

    — — — — — — — — —

geography   natural resources   crossroads   prosperous   kinship
savanna   culture   revenue   griot   clan

B. *Circle the word that makes sense in each sentence. Then write the word.*

1. Muslim traders from North Africa brought their religion, language, and (savanna, culture) to West Africa. _____

2. Kingdoms in West Africa grew (prosperous, crossroads) from trade in salt and gold. _____

3. If kinship groups shared a common ancestor, then they formed a larger group called a (griot, clan). _____

4. Desert, savanna, and rain forests make up the (natural resources, geography) of West Africa. _____

5. A (savanna, clan) is a grassy plain with few trees. _____

6. The kings of Ghana grew rich from the (kinship, revenue) they received from taxing traders. _____

7. Because of Ghana's location, it became a (prosperous, crossroads) of trade.
   _____

8. Gold was among the most valuable (geography, natural resources) of West Africa. _____

9. The foundation of many African societies was formed by (culture, kinship) groups. _____

10. In West Africa, a (revenue, griot) passed on stories of a clan's history.
    _____

WORD ROOT

The word **geography** comes from the Greek words **ge** and **graphein**. **Ge** means "earth," and **graphein** means "write."

geography   natural resources   crossroads   prosperous   kinship

savanna   culture   revenue   griot   clan

C. *Choose the correct vocabulary word to complete each sentence.*

1. Gold and salt made Ghana and Mali _____ centers of trade.

2. In the grassy plain of the _____ , few trees are found.

3. The two kinship groups formed a _____ because they shared the same great-grandfather.

4. Taxes are a source of _____ for governments.

5. Family relationships, or _____, were very important in West Africa.

6. West Africa's _____ includes the Niger River, which flows across the region.

7. African empires gained great wealth from trade in _____ such as gold and salt.

8. By passing on history through stories, a _____ plays a key role in African life.

9. Ghana rose to power because of its location at a _____ of trade.

10. The empire of Mali was influenced by the _____ of the Muslim traders, including their religion and language.

| geography | natural resources | crossroads | prosperous | kinship |
| savanna | culture | revenue | griot | clan |

D. *Use each pair of words in a sentence.*

1. griot, clan

   _____

   _____

   _____

2. savanna, geography

   _____

   _____

   _____

3. culture, kinship

   _____

   _____

   _____

4. crossroads, prosperous

   _____

   _____

   _____

5. revenue, natural resources

   _____

   _____

   _____

Write!

Write your response to the prompt on a separate sheet of paper. Use as many vocabulary words as you can in your writing.

Imagine you are a modern-day griot in West Africa. Tell the history of a clan or kinship group from your village that dates back to the Middle Ages.

How are you influenced by your friends and neighbors and by where you live? Read this selection to find out what influenced Japan's development.

Japan in the Middle Ages

Japan's Geography

Thousands of islands form the archipelago of Japan. An **archipelago** is a group or chain of islands. Surrounded by water, Japan was protected from invaders. The ocean **isolated**, or separated, Japan from the rest of Asia for centuries.

The traditional religion of Japan is called Shinto. **Shinto** is based on respect for nature and ancestors. In the Shinto religion, rivers, trees, mountains, and all other things in nature have their own divine spirits.

The Archipelago of Japan

Prince Shotoku

In A.D. 593, a young man named Shotoku became Japan's crown prince. Shotoku introduced many elements of Chinese culture to Japan. He formed a strong central government based on the ideas of Confucius. Confucius was a Chinese scholar. Shotoku used these ideas to create Japan's first constitution. A **constitution** is a written plan of government. The constitution gave all power to the emperor.

Prince Shotoku is shown here with his two sons.

Prince Shotoku also introduced Buddhism to Japan. Many people adopted Buddhism. They combined it with Shinto beliefs. One form of Japanese Buddhism is called **Zen**. Zen focuses on achieving inner peace.

Rise of a Military Society

Japan's central government and emperors remained strong for many centuries. Then, in the 1100s, they grew weak. **Daimyo**, Japanese lords with large estates, gained power. Violence increased as daimyo fought to gain more land, wealth, and power. They hired samurai for protection. A **samurai** was a highly skilled warrior. The samurai followed a strict code of honor, loyalty, and bravery.

Japan became a military society. The emperor was still at the top of Japanese society. But he did not have real power. A **shogun**, or military leader, ruled the country for the emperor. Shoguns ruled Japan until 1867.

This samurai warrior stops his enemies' arrows.

Japanese Arts

Japan has a long tradition in the arts. One form of Japanese drama dates back to early Shinto dances. Actors wore painted masks to express emotions. Another form of drama also developed. It is called kabuki. **Kabuki** combines singing and dancing, bold makeup, and elaborate costumes.

One of Japan's finest writers was Murasaki Shikibu. She lived at the emperor's court in the 800s. She wrote *The Tale of Genji*. It tells the story of a prince. Many people think it is the world's first novel, or long work of fiction. The Japanese also developed a new form of poetry. **Haiku** is a short poem arranged in three lines. Japanese poets often wrote about the beauty of nature in haiku.

Kabuki is still popular in Japan.

My Social Studies Vocabulary

Go to page 95 to list other words you have learned about Japan in the Middle Ages.

| archipelago | Shinto | Zen | samurai | kabuki |
| isolated | constitution | daimyo | shogun | haiku |

A. *Match each word with its meaning. Write the letter of the correct meaning on the line in front of each word.*

1. _____ constitution

2. _____ isolated

3. _____ daimyo

4. _____ kabuki

5. _____ shogun

6. _____ haiku

7. _____ Zen

8. _____ archipelago

9. _____ samurai

10. _____ Shinto

a. a traditional Japanese religion based on respect for nature and ancestors

b. a short poem arranged in three lines

c. a form of Japanese drama that combines singing, dancing, bold makeup, and elaborate costumes

d. a group or chain of islands

e. separated

f. a highly skilled Japanese warrior

g. a written plan of government

h. Japanese lords with large estates

i. a form of Japanese Buddhism that focuses on achieving inner peace

j. a military leader

| archipelago | Shinto | Zen | samurai | kabuki |
| isolated | constitution | daimyo | shogun | haiku |

B. *Choose and write the two words that best complete each sentence.*

| daimyo | shogun | Shinto | constitution |

1. The _____ gave all power to the emperor, but a military

    leader called a _____ became the actual ruler of Japan.

| isolated | kabuki | constitution | archipelago |

2. The islands that form the _____ of Japan kept the country

    _____ for centuries.

| Zen | haiku | Shinto | samurai |

3. Followers of _____ believe that trees and rivers have divine

    spirits, while followers of _____ try to achieve inner peace.

| shogun | samurai | daimyo | isolated |

4. To protect themselves and their large estates, _____ hired

    loyal and highly trained warriors called _____ .

| haiku | kabuki | archipelago | Zen |

5. Japan created new art forms, including a form of theater called

    _____ and a form of poetry called _____ .

WORD ROOT

The word **isolated** comes from the Latin word
insula, which means "island."

archipelago   Shinto   Zen   samurai   kabuki

isolated   constitution   daimyo   shogun   haiku

C. *Choose the correct vocabulary word to complete each sentence.*

1. Large estates brought wealth and power to _____ in Japanese society.

2. A Japanese form of poetry called _____ often expresses the beauty of nature.

3. As skilled warriors, _____ lived by a strict code of honor, loyalty, and bravery.

4. Bodies of water separate the _____ of Japan from the rest of Asia.

5. Respect for nature inspired the Japanese traditional religion known as _____ .

6. An actor performing in a _____ drama wears bold makeup and an elaborate costume.

7. Seas kept Japan _____ from China and Korea for centuries.

8. A form of Buddhism practiced in Japan is known as _____ .

9. Prince Shotoku used the ideas of a Chinese scholar to write Japan's _____ .

10. As a military leader, the _____ controlled large armies and had power over the emperor.

Japan in the Middle Ages

| archipelago | Shinto | Zen | samurai | kabuki |
| isolated | constitution | daimyo | shogun | haiku |

D. *Use each pair of words in a sentence.*

1. kabuki, haiku

   _____

   _____

   _____

2. daimyo, samurai

   _____

   _____

   _____

3. archipelago, isolated

   _____

   _____

   _____

4. constitution, shogun

   _____

   _____

   _____

5. Shinto, Zen

   _____

   _____

   _____

Write!

**Write your response to the prompt on a separate sheet of paper.
Use as many vocabulary words as you can in your writing.**

Imagine you are a Japanese poet. Write a diary entry recording your thoughts
and experiences about daily life in Japan in the Middle Ages.

LESSON 7

medieval   vassal   chivalry   serf   Magna Carta
feudalism   knight   manor   guild   parliament

*What words and images come to mind when you think about the
Middle Ages in Europe? Read this selection to find out what life
was like for people in Europe during the Middle Ages.*

Medieval Europe

An Unstable Time

The Middle Ages lasted from about 500 to about
1500. This time in history is also known as the
medieval period. In the early Middle Ages, a king
called Charlemagne built a great empire. After
Charlemagne died in 814, war and disorder spread
across the region.

*Charlemagne was one
of the most important
medieval kings.*

The Development of Feudalism

During this unstable time, people needed order
and protection. A new system of government called
feudalism emerged. Kings and lords were at the top
of the feudal system. They owned land and ruled
over others.

Each lord had a number of vassals. A **vassal** received land and
protection from a lord. In return, the vassal pledged his loyalty.
He also provided the lord with knights. A **knight** was an armored
warrior. Knights fought on horseback. They defended the lord and
his land. Knights lived by a code of behavior called **chivalry**.
According to this code, knights were supposed to be brave, loyal,
and kind.

Medieval Europe

The Role of the Manor

A lord's estate was called a **manor**. A manor included the lord's castle or home, a village and church, peasant homes, pastures, and farm fields. Peasants were poor people who worked the land. Most of them were serfs. A **serf** was tied to the land. If the lord sold a plot of land, the serf stayed with that land. Serfs could not marry, own property, or leave the manor without the lord's permission.

Find the manor house and the serfs' houses in this picture.

The Growth of Towns

Over time, feudalism broke down. As trade grew, towns formed. Some people were able to leave the land. They became merchants and craftspeople. In the towns these people formed guilds. A **guild** is a group of people with the same trade or craft. The guilds governed the towns. They also favored rule by a king instead of a lord.

Medieval England

In England, changes took place that are still important today. One of the most important documents of the Middle Ages was the Magna Carta. The **Magna Carta** is a list of political rights. It was written by England's nobles. King John signed it in 1215. One important right of the Magna Carta was trial by jury. The nobles also limited the power of the king. They set up a parliament. A **parliament** is a governing body made up of a group of representatives.

King John signed the Magna Carta, making it law.

My Social Studies Vocabulary

Go to page 96 to list other words you have learned about medieval Europe.

medieval	vassal	chivalry	serf	Magna Carta
feudalism	knight	manor	guild	parliament

A. *Fill in the blanks with the correct vocabulary word.*

1. a group formed by people with the same trade or craft

   — — — — —

2. having to do with the Middle Ages

   — — — — — — — —

3. an armored warrior who fought on horseback

   — — — — — —

4. a list of political rights written by England's nobles and signed by King John

   — — — — — — — — — —

5. a system of government that developed in the Middle Ages in Europe

   — — — — — — — — —

6. a code of behavior by which knights were expected to be brave, loyal, and kind

   — — — — — — — —

7. a governing body made up of a group of representatives

   — — — — — — — — — —

8. a lord's estate

   — — — — —

9. a person who received land and protection from a lord in return for loyalty

   — — — — — —

10. a peasant farmer who was tied to the land

    — — — —

medieval   vassal   chivalry   serf   Magna Carta
feudalism   knight   manor   guild   parliament

B. *Choose and write the two words that best complete each sentence.*

knight	feudalism	chivalry	vassal

1. The code of _____ called for a _____
   to be brave, loyal, and kind.

Magna Carta	manor	medieval	guild

2. In the unstable times of _____ Europe, a lord's
   _____ provided a safe place to live and work.

Magna Carta	parliament	chivalry	medieval

3. England's government was changed by a list of rights called the
   _____ and by a new governing body called a
   _____ .

manor	feudalism	vassal	serf

4. Under the system of _____ , a lord gave land and
   protection to a _____ in exchange for a pledge of loyalty.

knight	serf	guild	parliament

5. A _____ lived on the land, while a craftsperson in
   a _____ lived in town.

WORD ROOT

The word **medieval** comes from the Latin words
medium, which means "middle," and **aevum**,
which means "age."

medieval	vassal	chivalry	serf	Magna Carta
feudalism	knight	manor	guild	parliament

C. *Choose the correct vocabulary word to complete each sentence.*

1. The new governing body called _____ became an important step toward representative government.

2. In a special ceremony, a _____ pledged his loyalty to a lord in exchange for land and protection.

3. Life for a _____ was difficult and included long hours farming the land on the lord's estate.

4. Under the system of _____ , kings and lords were at the top of the social order and peasants were at the bottom.

5. Trial by jury was one of the rights guaranteed in the _____ .

6. During the Middle Ages, bakers, weavers, and shoemakers joined a _____ with others who shared their same craft or trade.

7. A fine example of building in the Middle Ages, the _____ castle on the hill was built in A.D. 1100.

8. The young boy dreamed of becoming a _____ dressed in armor and riding a horse into battle.

9. Few people had reason to leave the _____ because the land on the estate provided nearly everything that was needed.

10. To live by the code of _____ , a knight had to be brave even in the fiercest battles.

| medieval | vassal | chivalry | serf | Magna Carta |
| feudalism | knight | manor | guild | parliament |

D. *Use each pair of words in a sentence.*

1. manor, serf

   _____

   _____

   _____

2. Magna Carta, parliament

   _____

   _____

   _____

3. vassal, knight

   _____

   _____

   _____

4. medieval, guild

   _____

   _____

   _____

5. feudalism, chivalry

   _____

   _____

   _____

Write!

Write your response to the prompt on a separate sheet of paper.
Use as many vocabulary words as you can in your writing.

Imagine you are a lord or lady living in the Middle Ages. Write a letter to a friend discussing details of your life in feudal society.

Think about what you already know about feudalism and the role it played in the Middle Ages. During that time period, why do you think the Church also began to play such an important role in Europe? Read this selection to find out about the role of the Catholic Church in medieval Europe.

The Role of the Church in Medieval Europe

The Growth of the Catholic Church

During the Middle Ages, feudalism helped to restore order in Europe. People also turned to religion during this difficult time. As Christianity spread, the Roman Catholic Church began to play an important role. By 1050, most people in Western Europe had become Catholic.

The leader of the Roman Catholic Church was the **pope**. Below the pope were members of the clergy. The **clergy** were religious officials. Priests were one group of the clergy. A **priest** performed religious ceremonies. Monks were also important in the Church. Monks lived in a **monastery**. There they led quiet lives. They prayed and worshipped.

Monks in this monastery created books by hand, one by one.

The Role of the Church in Medieval Europe

Kings and Popes

For a long time, European kings and popes helped each other. But European kings and Church leaders grew more powerful. They argued over who was in charge. In 1073, Pope Gregory VII issued a **decree**, or order. The decree ordered kings to stop appointing Church officials. Emperor Henry IV of Germany was furious at the decree. He declared that Gregory VII was no longer pope. The struggle between kings and the pope for control of society continued a long time.

The Catholic Church and Society

Daily life in medieval Europe was built around the Catholic Church. Wealthy Church leaders, lords, and merchants built large new churches. A big, important church is called a **cathedral**.

A cathedral was a center of learning and faith.

Schools were founded at cathedrals. As cities grew, cathedral schools expanded and became universities. A **university** is a school of advanced learning. Universities educated and trained scholars in many subjects. These included grammar, speech, science, mathematics, and music. Teachers taught their students in Latin.

The Crusades

In 1071, an army of Muslim Turks captured Jerusalem. Jerusalem was a **sacred**, or holy, place to Christians, Jews, and Muslims. Christian pilgrims could no longer travel safely to Jerusalem. A **pilgrim** is a religious person who travels to a holy place.

The purpose of this Christian crusade was to take back the sacred city of Jerusalem.

In 1096, Pope Urban II launched a crusade against the Muslim Turks. A **crusade** is a military expedition. Over the next 200 years, Christian armies from Europe went on eight crusades. They wanted to take back the city of Jerusalem. Christian armies were successful at first. In 1099, the First Crusade captured Jerusalem. But the Europeans never had the support of the people living there. Muslims retook Jerusalem in 1187.

My Social Studies Vocabulary

Go to page 96 to list other words you have learned about the role of the Church in medieval Europe.

The Role of the Church in Medieval Europe

| pope | priest | decree | university | pilgrim |
| clergy | monastery | cathedral | sacred | crusade |

A. *Match each word with its meaning. Write the letter of the correct meaning on the line in front of each word.*

1. _____ decree

2. _____ priest

3. _____ university

4. _____ clergy

5. _____ sacred

6. _____ pilgrim

7. _____ pope

8. _____ cathedral

9. _____ crusade

10. _____ monastery

a. the leader of the Roman Catholic Church

b. religious officials

c. a place where monks lived quiet lives of prayer and worship

d. a member of the Catholic clergy who performed religious ceremonies

e. an order given by a ruler

f. a large, important church

g. a school of advanced learning

h. holy

i. a religious person who travels to a holy place

j. a Christian military expedition to Jerusalem in the Middle Ages

The Role of the Church in Medieval Europe

| pope | priest | decree | university | pilgrim |
| clergy | monastery | cathedral | sacred | crusade |

B. *Circle the word that makes sense in each sentence. Then write the word.*

1. Students at the (monastery, university) studied many different subjects in Latin.

   _____

2. A large, medieval (university, cathedral) was often the center of life in the city.

   _____

3. As leader of the Roman Catholic Church, the (pope, priest) had great power over people's lives in the Middle Ages. _____

4. A devout Christian hoped to visit the holy, or (pilgrim, sacred), city of Jerusalem before his death. _____

5. The pope's (crusade, decree), or order, caused a major conflict with Emperor Henry IV of Germany. _____

6. Priests and monks were two groups of religious officials that belonged to the (monastery, clergy). _____

7. Monks lived quiet lives of prayer in a (cathedral, monastery).

   _____

8. On his way to the holy city of Jerusalem, the (pilgrim, clergy) found the road difficult. _____

9. The pope called for Christian armies to go on a (decree, crusade) to recapture the holy city of Jerusalem. _____

10. After being appointed by the Church, the (sacred, priest) took up his duty of performing religious ceremonies. _____

WORD ROOT

The word **university** comes from the Latin word **universus**, which means "whole" or "entire."

pope	priest	decree	university	pilgrim
clergy	monastery	cathedral	sacred	crusade

C. *Choose the correct vocabulary word to complete each sentence.*

1. On his long journey to the holy city, the tired _____ stopped along the road to rest.

2. The king ignored the pope's _____ , which led to a major conflict with the Church.

3. In a medieval _____ , students studied grammar, mathematics, science, and music.

4. The political and spiritual leader of the Roman Catholic Church is the _____ .

5. Communion, marriage, and baptism were among the many religious ceremonies performed by a _____ in the Church.

6. The city of Jerusalem is considered a _____ place by Christians, Jews, and Muslims.

7. On the _____ to recapture Jerusalem, tens of thousands of Christian soldiers died.

8. The _____ was made up of different ranks of religious officials appointed by the Church.

9. In the quiet _____ , monks studied, prayed, and copied religious texts.

10. The wealthy merchants helped to pay for the construction of a _____ to replace the smaller church.

The Role of the Church in Medieval Europe

pope	priest	decree	university	pilgrim
clergy	monastery	cathedral	sacred	crusade

D. *Use each word in a sentence that shows you understand the meaning of the word.*

1. monastery _____

_____

2. pilgrim _____

_____

3. pope _____

_____

4. decree _____

_____

5. priest _____

_____

6. clergy _____

_____

7. crusade _____

_____

8. cathedral _____

_____

9. university _____

_____

10. sacred _____

_____

Write!

Write your response to the prompt on a separate sheet of paper. Use as many vocabulary words as you can in your writing.

Imagine you are a young person growing up in medieval Europe. Write a journal entry describing the role of the Church in your European town or city.

LESSON 9

Mesoamerica agriculture architecture tribute terrain

maize sacrifice legend conquistador quipu

What do you already know about the Mayan, Aztec, and Inca civilizations? Where did they develop? What were their great achievements? Read this selection to find out about the early civilizations of the Americas.

Early Civilizations of the Americas

Geography Shapes Ways of Life

Mesoamerica, or Middle America, lies between North and South America. It includes Mexico and Central America. This region has mountains, lowlands, and rain forests. The varied landscape provided many natural resources for the people of the region.

Fertile soil in some areas also made the region good for growing crops, such as maize. **Maize** is a type of corn used to make many kinds of foods. **Agriculture**, or farming, thrived. With more food, populations grew. These Mesoamerican groups developed into the Mayan and Aztec civilizations.

The Maya

Mayan society was divided into four classes: kings, nobles, peasants, and slaves. A king ruled each Mayan city. He acted as a priest in religious ceremonies. The Maya believed in many gods. Their religion sometimes called for **sacrifice**, or the killing of animals or humans to please the gods.

The Maya made statues of their gods and offered them sacrifices.

The Maya were known for their architecture. **Architecture** is the art of constructing buildings. Mayans built palaces, plazas, and huge ball courts. They also built pyramids topped with temples. By the 1400s, the Mayan civilization had come to a mysterious end.

The Aztecs

According to an Aztec **legend**, or story, an Aztec god told the Aztec people where to live. In 1325 they built the city of Tenochtitlán on an island in a lake. Today, this is Mexico City.

The Aztecs were fearsome warriors. They conquered neighboring peoples. The Aztecs demanded **tribute**, or a forced payment in goods, from these people. The Aztecs could not, however, defeat the Spanish. In 1521, conquistadors defeated the Aztec empire. A **conquistador** was a Spanish explorer and soldier who conquered native people.

The Inca

The Inca settled in the Andes of South America. The rugged **terrain,** or landscape, of these mountains made farming difficult. So Inca farmers cut steps into the mountains to create flat areas.

Inca rulers set up a highly organized government. An emperor was their supreme ruler. The Inca also built a huge network of roads in the mountains. These roads were important for communication and trade. The Inca kept track of trade and other records with a counting tool. It was called a quipu. A **quipu** was a set of knotted strings of different colors, which hung from a cord.

Like the Aztecs, the Inca had a large, powerful army. In 1532, however, Spanish conquistadors invaded Peru. By 1572, they had defeated the entire Inca empire.

Pyramids topped with temples were common in Mayan architecture.

This Inca man might be using a quipu to count the number of cattle he owns.

My Social Studies Vocabulary

Go to page 96 to list other words you have learned about the early civilizations of the Americas.

| Mesoamerica | agriculture | architecture | tribute | terrain |
| maize | sacrifice | legend | conquistador | quipu |

A. *Fill in the blanks with the correct vocabulary word.*

1. a forced payment in goods to a ruler

   — — — — — — —

2. a type of corn

   — — — — —

3. landscape

   — — — — — — —

4. the region that includes Mexico and Central America

   — — — — — — — — — — —

5. a counting tool made of knotted strings

   — — — — —

6. a Spanish explorer and soldier who conquered native people in the Americas

   — — — — — — — — — — — —

7. farming

   — — — — — — — — — — —

8. a story about the past

   — — — — — —

9. the practice of killing animals or humans to please the gods

   — — — — — — — — —

10. the art of constructing buildings

    — — — — — — — — — — — —

Early Civilizations of the Americas

| Mesoamerica | agriculture | architecture | tribute | terrain |
| maize | sacrifice | legend | conquistador | quipu |

B. *Circle the word that makes sense in each sentence. Then write the word.*

1. One of the most important crops in early American civilizations was a type of corn called (quipu, maize). _____

2. Palaces, plazas, and pyramids topped with temples are all examples of Mayan (terrain, architecture). _____

3. The Maya and Aztecs built their empires in a region known as (Mesoamerica, maize). _____

4. The Aztecs demanded (sacrifice, tribute) in goods such as gold and jade from the people they conquered. _____

5. Powerful weapons gave a Spanish (conquistador, Mesoamerica) the advantage when battling an Aztec warrior. _____

6. In the rugged mountain (agriculture, terrain) of Peru, Inca farmers cut steps into the mountainside to create more farmland. _____

7. According to an Aztec (tribute, legend), the sun and war god told the Aztec people where to build a new empire. _____

8. The Maya, Aztecs, and Inca based their societies on (agriculture, architecture), which helped their populations grow. _____

9. The Inca used a counting tool called a (quipu, conquistador) to keep track of births and deaths. _____

10. In a ceremony for a good harvest, the Aztecs would sometimes offer a human (legend, sacrifice) to the gods. _____

WORD **ROOT**

The word **tribute** comes from the Latin word **tribuere**, which originally meant "to pay" or "to divide among tribes."

Mesoamerica   agriculture   architecture   tribute   terrain

maize   sacrifice   legend   conquistador   quipu

C.   *Choose the correct vocabulary word to complete each sentence.*

1. The Inca did not have a system of writing, but they created a record-keeping
    system that used a tool called a _____ .

2. The basic crop of _____ was important to the
    Mayan civilization.

3. The Inca created a large empire in the high and rugged
    _____ of the Andes mountains.

4. The Spanish _____ wore armor, carried a musket,
    and rode on a horse into the Aztec territory.

5. Mayan cities were known for their magnificent _____ ,
    which included palaces, plazas, ball courts, and pyramids.

6. In Inca society, the priest offered the _____ of an animal
    for a good harvest.

7. The Aztecs created new techniques in _____ , such as
    raised garden beds that allowed them to grow many crops.

8. The Aztec emperor Montezuma demanded great payments of
    _____ from the peoples he conquered.

9. The region of _____ includes Mexico and Central
    America.

10. According to Aztec _____ , an eagle sitting on a cactus
    marked the location of the new Aztec home.

Mesoamerica	agriculture	architecture	tribute	terrain
maize	sacrifice	legend	conquistador	quipu

D. *Use each word in a sentence that shows you understand the meaning of the word.*

1. maize _____

   _____

2. terrain _____

   _____

3. tribute _____

   _____

4. architecture _____

   _____

5. sacrifice _____

   _____

6. legend _____

   _____

7. quipu _____

   _____

8. conquistador _____

   _____

9. agriculture _____

   _____

10. Mesoamerica _____

   _____

Write! _____

Write your response to the prompt on a separate sheet of paper.
Use as many vocabulary words as you can in your writing.

Imagine you are an archaeologist who has discovered the ruins of a long-lost city of the Mayan, Aztec, or Inca civilization. Write a letter to a fellow archaeologist describing what you have learned from your discovery.

classics   secular   urban   patron   printing press
humanism   Renaissance   appreciation   masterpiece   vernacular

Where do you come in contact with new ideas? How do new ideas spark your creativity? Read this selection to find out about the Renaissance, a period of new ideas and great creativity in Europe.

The Renaissance

Trade Opens Europe to New Ideas

Europe became more stable in the late Middle Ages. An ancient trade route reopened. The Silk Road stretched from Europe to China. Marco Polo, an Italian trader, told stories about his trip along the Silk Road. His stories led to increased trade with China and other parts of Asia.

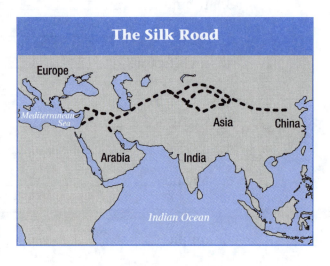

The growth of trade had another effect. It introduced people to different cultures and new ideas. Europeans turned once again to the **classics**. These are the works of ancient Greek and Roman writers. This led to a new way of thought called humanism. **Humanism** stressed the importance of human beings and human achievement. People's interests became more **secular**, or related to the world rather than to the Church. Humanism sparked people's desire to create. It also sparked the **Renaissance**. This was a period of renewed creativity and great achievements in the arts.

The Renaissance

The Renaissance Begins in Italy

The Renaissance began in Italy around 1300. Italy's northern cities had become very wealthy from trade. Florence, Venice, and Milan became large **urban**, or city, centers. In these cities, a wealthy upper class had time to study the classics. They also developed an **appreciation**, or understanding, of the arts.

The citizens of Florence had a great appreciation of art.

Florence was the most important city of the early Renaissance. It was one of the largest cities in Europe. Florence had gained great wealth from trading and banking. The Medici, a powerful banking family, ruled Florence. The Medici became patrons of Italy's Renaissance artists. A **patron** gives money to help someone. With the help of a patron, artists could spend their time creating masterpieces. A **masterpiece** is an outstanding work of art.

Renaissance Ideas Spread

The growth of trade and cities helped to spread Renaissance ideas. As in Italy, wealthy merchants in northern Europe became patrons. They supported local artists and writers.

The printing press also helped to spread Renaissance ideas. The **printing press** was a machine. It pressed paper against inked, moveable type. The printing press made it possible to produce many books quickly. Books became less expensive, so more people could buy them. More people learned to read. Before the printing press, most writers wrote in Latin. Now they wanted books written in the vernacular. The **vernacular** is someone's native language. The use of the vernacular made Renaissance ideas available to readers throughout Europe.

The printing press made it easier to share new ideas.

My Social Studies Vocabulary

Go to page 97 to list other words you have learned about the Renaissance.

The Renaissance

classics   secular   urban   patron   printing press
humanism   Renaissance   appreciation   masterpiece   vernacular

A. *Match each word with its meaning. Write the letter of the correct meaning on the line in front of each word.*

1. _____ vernacular

2. _____ urban

3. _____ Renaissance

4. _____ patron

5. _____ secular

6. _____ classics

7. _____ humanism

8. _____ printing press

9. _____ appreciation

10. _____ masterpiece

a. a person who helps an artist or writer by giving money

b. a machine that pressed paper against inked, moveable type

c. an outstanding work of art

d. a way of thought that stressed the importance of human beings and human achievement

e. a person's native language

f. a period in Europe of renewed creativity and great achievements in the arts

g. understanding

h. relating to a city

i. the works of ancient Greek and Roman writers

j. related to things that are not religious

classics	secular	urban	patron	printing press
humanism	Renaissance	appreciation	masterpiece	vernacular

B. *Circle the word that makes sense in each sentence. Then write the word.*

1. The (vernacular, printing press) made it possible to produce books more quickly. _____

2. A new way of thought called (humanism, secular) encouraged a spirit of learning and artistic exploration. _____

3. Renaissance merchants developed an (urban, appreciation) for the arts. _____

4. The Medici family was an important (patron, printing press) of the arts in Florence. _____

5. To a person in France, French is the (classics, vernacular). _____

6. As life became more (secular, urban), people became more interested in worldly affairs. _____

7. The period in Europe of renewed creativity and great achievements in the arts is called the (vernacular, Renaissance). _____

8. The city of Florence became a wealthy and important (urban, appreciation) center. _____

9. Everyone agreed that this painting was the artist's (patron, masterpiece). _____

10. To educate themselves, Europeans read Greek (classics, Renaissance). _____

WORD ROOT

The word **urban** comes from the Latin root **urbs**, which means "city."

classics   secular   urban   patron   printing press

humanism   Renaissance   appreciation   masterpiece   vernacular

C. *Choose the correct vocabulary word to complete each sentence.*

1. The outstanding painting created by a Renaissance artist is a _____ that now hangs in a museum.

2. The growth of trade turned Florence, Venice, and Milan into busy _____ centers.

3. A renewed interest in learning led Europeans to study the _____ of the ancient past.

4. People wanted to read books written in the _____ instead of Latin.

5. Followers of _____ focus on human achievement.

6. The wealthy upper classes studied classical ideas, and their _____ for the arts grew.

7. Books became more widely available following the invention of the _____ .

8. A period of renewed achievement in the arts known as the _____ began in Italy around 1300.

9. Religious matters may not be important to a _____ person.

10. As a _____ of the arts, the wealthy noble supported the work of many painters in Florence.

classics	secular	urban	patron	printing press
humanism	Renaissance	appreciation	masterpiece	vernacular

D. *Use each pair of words in a sentence.*

1. classics, Renaissance

   _____

   _____

   _____

2. humanism, secular

   _____

   _____

   _____

3. urban, patron

   _____

   _____

   _____

4. printing press, vernacular

   _____

   _____

   _____

5. masterpiece, appreciation

   _____

   _____

   _____

Write!

**Write your response to the prompt on a separate sheet of paper.
Use as many vocabulary words as you can in your writing.**

Imagine you are a wealthy merchant living in Florence during the Renaissance. Write a journal entry describing how Renaissance ideas have affected your daily life.

What do you already know about some of the great artists of the Renaissance? Why are their works of art and other achievements still valued today? Read this selection to find out about the leading figures and achievements of the Renaissance.

Leading Figures and Achievements of the Renaissance

New Ideas and Techniques

Renaissance art differed from the art of the Middle Ages. Medieval artists focused on religious subjects. Renaissance artists also showed religious subjects sometimes. But they showed these subjects and others in a more lifelike way.

Renaissance artists also used new techniques. A **technique** is a method used to make something. The most important new technique was perspective. **Perspective** makes objects on a flat surface seem to have distance and depth. Another new technique was proportion. **Proportion** shows the relationship between

Renaissance artist Leonardo da Vinci used perspective to give this scene depth.

objects in terms of size and shape. Because of perspective and proportion, Renaissance works of art looked more realistic.

Leading Figures and Their Masterpieces

In Italy, two Renaissance artists towered above the others. They were Leonardo da Vinci and Michelangelo. Da Vinci's most famous paintings are *The Last Supper* and the *Mona Lisa*. The *Mona Lisa* is believed to be a portrait of a wealthy merchant's wife. A **portrait** is a painting or drawing of a person. Da Vinci had many apprentices. An **apprentice** is a beginner in an art or a trade.

The woman in this portrait smiles as if she knows a secret.

Michelangelo produced a large number of artworks, including marble statues. Michelangelo's greatest achievement was a huge painting. It covered the ceiling of the Sistine Chapel in Rome. The painting was a commission from Pope Julius II. A **commission** is an order for a work of art.

The **literature**, or written works, of the Renaissance also broke new ground. Renaissance writers focused on the lives of human beings. The most famous writer of the Northern Renaissance was William Shakespeare. He was a poet and playwright. A **playwright** is a person who writes plays.

Advances in Many Fields

Renaissance scientists were also curious about the world they lived in. Renaissance scientists made advances in **astronomy**, the study of the stars and planets. This led to new ideas about the universe.

One of the best scientists of the Renaissance was the great artist Leonardo da Vinci. He filled notebooks with detailed drawings of many subjects. His accurate drawings advanced the science of anatomy. **Anatomy** is the study of the human body.

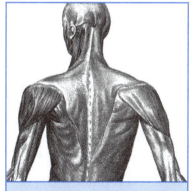

Leonardo da Vinci's drawings of human anatomy showed details of bones and muscles.

My Social Studies Vocabulary

Go to page 97 to list other words you have learned about leading figures and achievements of the Renaissance.

Leading Figures and Achievements of the Renaissance

| technique | proportion | apprentice | literature | astronomy |
| perspective | portrait | commission | playwright | anatomy |

A. *Circle the word that best answers each question.*

1. I am a person who writes plays. Who am I?

    portrait   playwright   literature

2. I am a beginner in an art or a trade. Who am I?

    apprentice   anatomy   commission

3. I am the study of the human body. What am I?

    proportion   astronomy   anatomy

4. I am a method used to make something. What am I?

    perspective   playwright   technique

5. I am written works. What am I?

    playwright   technique   literature

6. I am a technique in art that shows the relationship between objects in terms of size and shape. What am I?

    perspective   proportion   portrait

7. I am the study of the stars and planets. What am I?

    anatomy   perspective   astronomy

8. I am a painting or drawing of a person. What am I?

    technique   portrait   proportion

9. I am a technique in art that makes objects on a flat surface appear to have distance and depth. What am I?

    proportion   astronomy   perspective

10. I am an order for a work of art to be created. What am I?

    commission   portrait   apprentice

Leading Figures and Achievements of the Renaissance

technique   proportion   apprentice   literature   astronomy

perspective   portrait   commission   playwright   anatomy

B. *Circle the word that makes sense in each sentence. Then write the word.*

1. Renaissance artists made objects on a flat surface appear to have distance and depth by using (perspective, proportion). _____

2. *Romeo and Juliet* is one of the plays written by the (apprentice, playwright) William Shakespeare. _____

3. Renaissance scientists learned more about (astronomy, anatomy) by studying the stars and planets. _____

4. The Renaissance artist discovered a new (perspective, technique), or method of making something. _____

5. A Renaissance artist might hope to be offered a (literature, commission) for a new painting. _____

6. Michelangelo used (commission, proportion) to show the relationship between objects. _____

7. By studying (anatomy, astronomy), Renaissance scientists learned more about the human body. _____

8. In their written works, or (technique, literature), Renaissance writers showed an understanding of human nature. _____

9. The (anatomy, apprentice) mixed the paints and cleaned the brushes for the master artist. _____

10. In a famous (literature, portrait) called the *Mona Lisa*, da Vinci painted the woman's face with a mysterious smile. _____

WORD ROOT

The word **perspective** comes from the Latin word **specere**, which means "to look."

technique	proportion	apprentice	literature	astronomy
perspective	portrait	commission	playwright	anatomy

C. *Choose the correct vocabulary word to complete each sentence.*

1. The young _____ hoped one day to be like his teacher, Leonardo da Vinci.

2. Shakespeare wrote comedies and tragedies and became a popular _____ in England.

3. Renaissance painters used a new _____ to move away from the flat painting of medieval art.

4. During the Renaissance, scientists learned more about the universe by studying _____ .

5. Renaissance _____ broke new ground as writers created realistic characters.

6. Leonardo da Vinci studied _____ in order to learn more about how the human body worked.

7. The technique known as _____ creates the appearance of three dimensions through distance and depth.

8. Art historians think the woman in the _____ is the wife of a wealthy merchant.

9. Michelangelo's painting on the ceiling of the Sistine Chapel was a _____ from Pope Julius II.

10. Because of perspective and _____ , objects in Renaissance works of art looked more realistic.

Leading Figures and Achievements of the Renaissance

technique	proportion	apprentice	literature	astronomy
perspective	portrait	commission	playwright	anatomy

D. *Use each word in a sentence that shows you understand the meaning of each word.*

1. playwright _____

_____

2. portrait _____

_____

3. apprentice _____

_____

4. anatomy _____

_____

5. technique _____

_____

6. commission _____

_____

7. perspective _____

_____

8. astronomy _____

_____

9. literature _____

_____

10. proportion _____

_____

Write! _____

Write your response to the prompt on a separate sheet of paper. Use as many vocabulary words as you can in your writing.

Imagine you are the master Renaissance artist Leonardo da Vinci. Write a journal entry in your notebook describing what inspires your work and your interest in many subjects.

indulgence   protest   Reformation   interpret   heretic
faith   public   Protestant   seminary   Inquisition

Have you ever wanted to reform, or change, something? Why? How would you go about making changes? Read this selection to find out about some of the changes caused by the Reformation in Europe.

The Reformation

Calls for Reform

During the 1400s, people began to question many practices of the Catholic Church. Many Catholics questioned the pope's power. They also did not like the way the Church earned its money. The Church placed heavy taxes on peasants. People objected most, however, to the sale of indulgences. An **indulgence** was a pardon for a person's sins. The idea that forgiveness could be bought angered people. Catholics demanded a change. They wanted the Church to reform and focus on spiritual matters.

This image shows the pope selling indulgences to pardon sins.

Luther's Ideas Challenge the Church

In the early 1500s, a monk named Martin Luther challenged the Church. Luther opposed the sale of indulgences. He also disagreed with many Church teachings. For example, the Church taught that people would be saved if they performed good deeds. Luther believed that people could be saved only through their faith. **Faith** is belief in God. Luther listed each **protest**, or disagreement, in his Ninety-Five Theses. He then made his list of protests **public**, or known to all. He nailed them to a church door.

Martin Luther's actions upset Church leaders. Many people, however, supported Luther's ideas. They joined the movement against the Catholic Church. This movement was the **Reformation**. A Christian who broke from the Catholic Church was known as a **Protestant**.

Martin Luther posted his protests on a church door.

The Protestant Reformation Grows

Luther's ideas spread across Europe. The printing press played a key role. Printers began producing Bibles in local languages. People could read and **interpret**, or explain the meaning of, the Bible on their own. They did not need the Catholic clergy to explain the Bible's meaning to them. Leaders of the Catholic Church feared that people would develop their own religious ideas. Church leaders saw this as a threat to their power.

The Counter Reformation

Over time, the Catholic Church made some reforms. It set rules for the clergy. It also set up seminaries. A **seminary** is a school for training priests. Priests helped to spread Catholicism across the world.

The Church also took steps to stop heretics. A **heretic** is a person who holds a belief that is different from what is accepted. This effort became known as the Counter Reformation. The Church established the Inquisition. The **Inquisition** was a court that investigated people accused of non-Catholic beliefs. People who were found guilty of being heretics received horrible punishments.

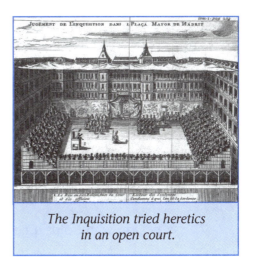

The Inquisition tried heretics in an open court.

My Social Studies Vocabulary

Go to page 97 to list other words you have learned about the Reformation.

The Reformation

71

indulgence	protest	Reformation	interpret	heretic
faith	public	Protestant	seminary	Inquisition

A. *Fill in the blanks with the correct vocabulary word.*

1. a school for training priests

   — — — — — — — —

2. a religious movement against the Catholic Church

   — — — — — — — — — — —

3. a court established by the Catholic Church to investigate people accused of non-Catholic beliefs

   — — — — — — — — — — —

4. belief in God

   — — — — —

5. an expression of disagreement

   — — — — — — —

6. a pardon for a person's sins

   — — — — — — — — — —

7. a person who holds a belief different from what is accepted

   — — — — — — —

8. a Christian who broke away from the Catholic Church

   — — — — — — — — — —

9. to explain the meaning of

   — — — — — — — — —

10. known to all

   — — — — — —

| indulgence | protest | Reformation | interpret | heretic |
| faith | public | Protestant | seminary | Inquisition |

B. *Circle the word that makes sense in each sentence. Then write the word.*

1. Martin Luther led a (seminary, protest) against the Catholic Church.

   _____

2. A person who was accused of being a (heretic, seminary) faced a severe punishment if found guilty. _____

3. Martin Luther believed that only (public, faith) in God could lead to salvation.

   _____

4. Many people believe the religious movement called the (Reformation, Inquisition) began with Martin Luther. _____

5. A Catholic could buy an (Inquisition, indulgence) if he or she wanted a sin to be pardoned. _____

6. The court of the (Inquisition, Reformation) accused many people of having non-Catholic beliefs. _____

7. Church leaders did not want people to (interpret, protest) the Bible on their own. _____

8. A Christian who broke away from the Catholic Church became known as a (Protestant, faith). _____

9. The printing press was an important tool in making Luther's ideas (heretic, public). _____

10. To become a priest, a student studied at a (seminary, Reformation).

    _____

WORD ROOT

The word **Reformation** comes from the Latin root **reformare**, which means "to form again."

The Reformation

indulgence	protest	Reformation	interpret	heretic
faith	public	Protestant	seminary	Inquisition

C. *Choose the correct vocabulary word to complete each sentence.*

1. Because they could read the Bible on their own, people did not need the clergy to _____ it for them.

2. By making his ideas _____ , Luther put himself in danger.

3. Martin Luther believed that an _____ should not be bought or sold.

4. Supporters of the _____ opposed many practices of the Catholic Church.

5. Luther's _____ in God remained strong.

6. One _____ made by Luther was against the sale of indulgences.

7. Many young men, hoping to become priests, attended the _____ .

8. A person who was a _____ belonged to a new branch of Christianity.

9. If a person held non-Catholic beliefs, he or she was considered a _____ by the Church.

10. The Church tried to stop heretics by establishing the court of the _____ .

The Reformation

| indulgence | protest | Reformation | interpret | heretic |
| faith | public | Protestant | seminary | Inquisition |

D. *Use each word in a sentence that shows you understand the meaning of each word.*

1. faith _____

   _____

2. indulgence _____

   _____

3. heretic _____

   _____

4. public _____

   _____

5. Inquisition _____

   _____

6. protest _____

   _____

7. interpret _____

   _____

8. Reformation _____

   _____

9. seminary _____

   _____

10. Protestant _____

   _____

Write!

Write your response to the prompt on a separate sheet of paper.
Use as many vocabulary words as you can in your writing.

Imagine you are living in Europe during the Reformation. Write a letter to a friend describing the changes you see taking place and how the Reformation has affected your life.

LESSON 13

theory   revolution   telescope   microscope   scientific method
orbit   heliocentric   gravity   thermometer   hypothesis

Have you ever made a discovery or come across a new idea that changed the way you look at the world? Read this selection to find out about some of the new ideas and discoveries of the Scientific Revolution.

The Scientific Revolution

Old and New Views of the World

Long ago, the Greek thinker Aristotle developed a theory. A **theory** is an explanation of how or why something happens. Aristotle claimed Earth was the center of the universe. Another scientist named Ptolemy agreed. He said that planets and stars move in an **orbit**, or path, around Earth. Their theories shaped people's thinking for more than one thousand years.

In the 1500s, the Renaissance sparked a new interest in science. Europeans began to question old ideas. They used math and close observation to develop new ideas. This led to a **revolution**, or major change, in science. This period is known as the Scientific Revolution.

A math scholar named Copernicus led the Scientific Revolution. He challenged Ptolemy's theory. Copernicus claimed that Earth, the stars, and other planets moved around the sun. His new theory was a **heliocentric**, or sun-centered, view of the universe.

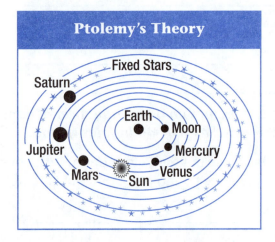

Ptolemy's Theory

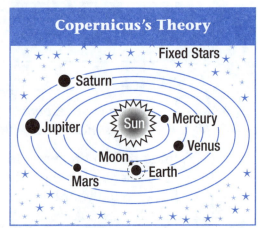

Copernicus's Theory

The Scientific Revolution

New Discoveries and Inventions

Scientists made new discoveries in many fields. The Italian scientist Galileo was the first person to use a telescope. A **telescope** is an instrument that makes things that are far away look bigger. Galileo's studies supported Copernicus' theory.

The English scientist Sir Isaac Newton defined gravity. **Gravity** is the force that causes objects to have weight and move toward each other. Newton believed that gravity acted on all objects in the universe in the same way. Gravity causes an apple to fall to the ground. Gravity also holds the planets in their orbit.

New instruments were invented. They helped scientists observe and measure things more carefully. A Dutch scientist invented the microscope. A **microscope** is an instrument that makes very small things look bigger. Galileo invented the thermometer. A **thermometer** is an instrument that measures how hot or cold something is.

Galileo used this telescope to study the night sky.

The Scientific Method

The English thinker Francis Bacon also influenced science. He developed the **scientific method**. This is an organized approach to scientific investigation. The scientific method is made up of a series of steps. In the first step, a scientist observes and describes the facts of a subject. Next, a scientist uses the facts to form a hypothesis. A **hypothesis** is an unproved explanation of the facts. To test whether a hypothesis is true, a scientist performs experiments.

Francis Bacon's scientific method changed the way in which people developed explanations of the unknown.

My Social Studies Vocabulary

Go to page 98 to list other words you have learned about the Scientific Revolution.

| theory | revolution | telescope | microscope | scientific method |
| orbit | heliocentric | gravity | thermometer | hypothesis |

A. *Circle the word that best answers each question.*

1. I am an instrument that makes things that are far away look bigger. What am I?

   microscope   telescope   thermometer

2. I am an organized approach to scientific investigation. What am I?

   scientific method   hypothesis   theory

3. I cause objects to have weight and move toward each other. What am I?

   orbit   revolution   gravity

4. I am an explanation of how or why something happens. What am I?

   hypothesis   theory   scientific method

5. I am an instrument that measures how hot or cold something is. What am I?

   thermometer   microscope   telescope

6. I am a major change. What am I?

   heliocentric   theory   revolution

7. I am a sun-centered view of the universe. What am I?

   orbit   heliocentric   hypothesis

8. I am an instrument that makes very small things look bigger. What am I?

   telescope   microscope   thermometer

9. I am an unproved explanation of the facts. What am I?

   hypothesis   gravity   scientific method

10. I am the path of one object around another in space. What am I?

   heliocentric   theory   orbit

theory   revolution   telescope   microscope   scientific method

orbit   heliocentric   gravity   thermometer   hypothesis

B. *Choose and write the two words that best complete each sentence.*

| theory | hypothesis | revolution | scientific method |

1. Francis Bacon developed the _____ , which uses facts to

   form a _____ about a subject.

| microscope | thermometer | heliocentric | telescope |

2. You can view distant planets and stars with a _____ , but

   you need a _____ to see very small objects.

| scientific method | orbit | revolution | theory |

3. Ptolemy built on Aristotle's _____ by claiming that planets

   and stars revolve in an _____ around Earth.

| revolution | orbit | heliocentric | hypothesis |

4. One of the new ideas that led to a _____ in science was that

   the universe was _____ , or sun-centered.

| thermometer | hypothesis | telescope | gravity |

5. _____ is a force that causes objects to have weight, and a

   _____ is an instrument that measures how hot or cold

   something is.

WORD ROOT

The word **gravity** comes from the Latin root **gravis**, which means "heavy."

theory   revolution   telescope   microscope   scientific method

orbit   heliocentric   gravity   thermometer   hypothesis

C. *Choose the correct vocabulary word to complete each sentence.*

1. Ptolemy claimed that each planet and star moves in an _____ around Earth.

2. Galileo was the first person to use a _____ to study the stars and planets.

3. Francis Bacon's _____ is still used in scientific research today.

4. Copernicus claimed that the universe was _____ , and Earth was not the center of the universe.

5. Galileo developed new scientific instruments, including the _____ , which measures how hot or cold something is.

6. Newton believed that _____ acted on all objects throughout the universe in the same way.

7. Scientists can observe very small objects more carefully using a _____ .

8. Aristotle developed a _____ that Earth was the center of the universe.

9. A scientist performs experiments to test if a _____ is true.

10. As people began to question old ideas, a _____ took place in the way people understood science.

theory	revolution	telescope	microscope	scientific method
orbit	heliocentric	gravity	thermometer	hypothesis

D. *Use each pair of words in a sentence.*

1. microscope, thermometer

   _____

   _____

   _____

2. gravity, orbit

   _____

   _____

   _____

3. theory, heliocentric

   _____

   _____

   _____

4. scientific method, hypothesis

   _____

   _____

   _____

5. telescope, revolution

   _____

   _____

   _____

 Write!

Write your response to the prompt on a separate sheet of paper.
Use as many vocabulary words as you can in your writing.

Imagine you are a young scientist living during the Scientific Revolution.
Write a journal entry describing how new ideas and inventions are
influencing your life and scientific research.

navigator   cartographer   astrolabe   Columbian Exchange   commerce
sponsor   caravel   latitude   colony   capitalism

If you could travel anywhere in the world, where would you go? How would you get there? How might tools of modern technology be helpful to you? Read this selection to find out about some of the great voyages that took place during the Age of Exploration.

The Age of Exploration

Great Voyages of Discovery

In the 1400s, Europeans wanted spices, silks, and other goods from Asia. This spurred them to look for sea routes to Asia. Portugal led the way. Portuguese ships sailed east. They went around Africa all the way to India. They set up many trading posts.

The Italian navigator Christopher Columbus had a different idea. He would sail west. A **navigator** directs the route of a ship. The king and queen of Spain became his sponsors. A **sponsor** is a person who gives money to support a

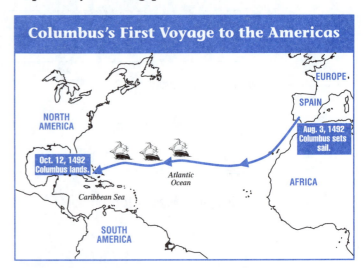

project. In 1492, Columbus' ships crossed the Atlantic Ocean. They landed, not in Asia, but on islands in the Caribbean Sea. Columbus claimed them for Spain. Then he sailed back with gold and pearls. He did not know he had discovered the Americas.

In 1519, Ferdinand Magellan of Portugal made another great voyage. He was the first to sail completely around the world.

New Technology

The Portuguese were the best cartographers at the time. A **cartographer** is a mapmaker. Their maps and other new tools helped to advance exploration. A Portuguese ship called a **caravel** had special sails. They were helpful on long voyages. The compass helped sailors keep track of direction. Sailors also used an instrument called an **astrolabe**. It found their ship's latitude. **Latitude** is a distance north or south of the equator.

This early astrolabe helped sailors to figure out their ship's latitude.

Effects of Exploration

New trade routes led to a worldwide exchange of goods and ideas. The **Columbian Exchange** was the movement of people, plants, animals, and diseases between the Eastern and Western hemispheres. This exchange began after Columbus sailed to the Americas.

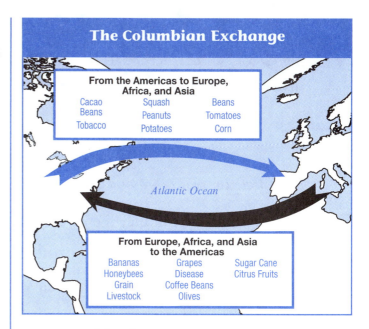

The Columbian Exchange

From the Americas to Europe, Africa, and Asia

Cacao	Squash	Beans
Beans	Peanuts	Tomatoes
Tobacco	Potatoes	Corn

Atlantic Ocean

From Europe, Africa, and Asia to the Americas

Bananas	Grapes	Sugar Cane
Honeybees	Disease	Citrus Fruits
Grain	Coffee Beans	
Livestock	Olives	

As worldwide trade increased, European countries set up colonies. A **colony** is a place controlled by another country. The natural resources of these colonies provided wealth to European countries.

Changes in Europe's Economy

During this period, commerce expanded. **Commerce** is the buying and selling of goods in large amounts over long distances. Capitalism also began to emerge. **Capitalism** is an economic system in which private owners control and use resources for profit.

My Social Studies Vocabulary

Go to page 98 to list other words you have learned about the Age of Exploration.

| navigator | cartographer | astrolabe | Columbian Exchange | commerce |
| sponsor | caravel | latitude | colony | capitalism |

A. *Circle the word that best answers each question.*

1. I am an instrument once used to find a ship's latitude. What am I?

   caravel   astrolabe   navigator

2. I am a person who gives money to support a project. Who am I?

   cartographer   navigator   sponsor

3. I am an economic system in which private owners control and use resources for profit. What am I?

   capitalism   commerce   Columbian Exchange

4. I am a mapmaker. Who am I?

   navigator   cartographer   astrolabe

5. I am the distance north or south of the equator. What am I?

   latitude   Columbian Exchange   caravel

6. I am a place that is controlled by another country. What am I?

   sponsor   capitalism   colony

7. I am a person who directs the route of a ship. Who am I?

   cartographer   sponsor   navigator

8. I am a ship with special sails designed for long voyages. What am I?

   caravel   astrolabe   latitude

9. I am the buying and selling of goods in large amounts over long distances. What am I?

   capitalism   commerce   colony

10. I am the movement of people, plants, animals, and diseases between the Eastern and Western hemispheres. What am I?

    commerce   capitalism   Columbian Exchange

The Age of Exploration

navigator   cartographer   astrolabe   Columbian Exchange   commerce
sponsor   caravel   latitude   colony   capitalism

B. *Circle the word that makes sense in each sentence. Then write the word.*

1. Spain set up a (caravel, colony) in the Americas, where Columbus had landed. _____

2. After finding out their ship's (latitude, astrolabe), sailors knew how far north or south of the equator they were. _____

3. As (navigator, sponsor), Columbus directed the ship to sail west. _____

4. Unfortunately, disease was one of the things that moved between hemispheres in the (commerce, Columbian Exchange). _____

5. Overseas trade and wealth from colonies led to the growth of a new economic system called (capitalism, colony). _____

6. Maps made by a (navigator, cartographer) were helpful tools in exploration. _____

7. The buying and selling of goods in large amounts over long distances is called (commerce, capitalism). _____

8. The (cartographer, sponsor) of the trip hoped to make money. _____

9. The special sails of the (latitude, caravel) were designed for long voyages. _____

10. Sailors used an instrument called the (caravel, astrolabe) to find their ship's latitude. _____

WORD ROOT

The word **astrolabe** comes from the Greek word **astron**, which means "star."

| navigator | cartographer | astrolabe | Columbian Exchange | commerce |
| sponsor | caravel | latitude | colony | capitalism |

C. *Choose the correct vocabulary word to complete each sentence.*

1. The map made by the _____ showed the west coast of Africa.

2. Under the economic system of _____ , private owners control and use resources for profit.

3. Christopher Columbus was the _____ for three ships that sailed across the Atlantic Ocean.

4. New foods came to Europe as part of the _____ .

5. The buying and selling of goods in large amounts over long distances is called _____ .

6. Columbus could afford to sail three ships across the Atlantic Ocean because he had a _____ for the voyage.

7. Sailors used the ship's _____ to find their distance from the equator.

8. The sailors wished they had a _____ for the long voyage.

9. The natural resources of a _____ provided wealth to the country that controlled it.

10. A distance north or south of the equator is called _____ .

The Age of Exploration

navigator   cartographer   astrolabe   Columbian Exchange   commerce
sponsor   caravel   latitude   colony   capitalism

D. Use each word in a sentence that shows you understand the meaning of the word.

1. caravel _____

_____

2. commerce _____

_____

3. Columbian Exchange _____

_____

4. navigator _____

_____

5. latitude _____

_____

6. capitalism _____

_____

7. sponsor _____

_____

8. astrolabe _____

_____

9. cartographer _____

_____

10. colony _____

_____

Write! _____

***Write your response to the prompt on a separate sheet of paper.
Use as many vocabulary words as you can in your writing.***

Imagine you are a sailor living during the 1400s, when the new era of exploration began. Write a journal entry describing one of your voyages overseas.

LESSON 15

rationalism   philosopher   liberty   independent   justice
Enlightenment   natural rights   democracy   equality   guarantee

What key ideas have shaped the democracy in which you live? What rights do you have as a citizen of a democracy? Read this selection to find out about the Enlightenment—an era that led to great changes in society and government.

The Enlightenment

Roots of the Enlightenment

Ancient Greek and Roman thinkers used research to answer questions and solve problems. **Rationalism** is the use of reason to understand the world. In the 1500s, Europeans rediscovered this method of thinking. They used reason to question old beliefs. They made new discoveries about the world. In the 1600s and

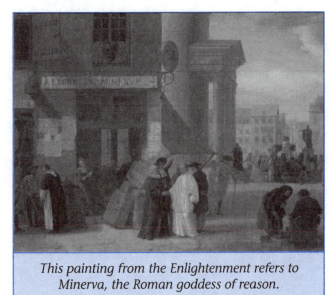

This painting from the Enlightenment refers to Minerva, the Roman goddess of reason.

1700s, European thinkers used reason to understand human nature and society. This marked the beginning of the **Enlightenment**. The ideas of this era would lead to great changes in society and government.

Philosophers and Ideas

Many philosophers influenced the ideas of the Enlightenment. A **philosopher** is a thinker who seeks wisdom. These philosophers used reason to solve problems and make society better.

The English philosopher John Locke argued that people are born with **natural rights**. These are the rights to life, liberty, and property. **Liberty** is freedom. Locke believed the government should protect these rights. He also noted the some governments did not protect these rights. If they did not, people had the right to set up a new government.

John Locke's ideas of natural rights and liberty were the seeds of our democracy.

Philosopher Jean-Jacques Rousseau believed that people are basically good.

The French philosopher Jean-Jacques Rousseau argued that the best system of government was a democracy. In a **democracy**, all citizens share in running the government.

The Spread of Enlightenment Ideas

Enlightenment ideas swept across Europe. Benjamin Franklin and Thomas Jefferson visited Europe. They agreed with Enlightenment ideas. They took these ideas back home to the colonies.

In America, conflict between the colonists and Great Britain was growing. The colonists wanted to be independent. **Independent** means free of being ruled by another country. Jefferson wrote the Declaration of Independence. It declared that the American colonies were independent from Britain. Jefferson used ideas about liberty, equality, and justice in his writing. **Equality** means having the same rights as other people. **Justice** means having fair laws. The document was signed on July 4, 1776. The colonies fought and won the American Revolution. They became an independent nation.

Americans used Enlightenment ideas again when forming their new government. They wanted a government that would **guarantee**, or make sure, the rights of its citizens. The democracy formed in America became a model for other countries.

The Declaration of Independence claimed that colonists had rights to liberty, equality, and justice.

My Social Studies Vocabulary

Go to page 98 to list other words you have learned about the Enlightenment.

rationalism   philosopher   liberty   independent   justice
Enlightenment   natural rights   democracy   equality   guarantee

A. *Match each word with its meaning. Write the letter of the correct meaning on the line in front of each word.*

1. _____ liberty

2. _____ equality

3. _____ democracy

4. _____ guarantee

5. _____ rationalism

6. _____ justice

7. _____ philosopher

8. _____ independent

9. _____ Enlightenment

10. _____ natural rights

a. the use of reason to understand the world

b. a period in which European thinkers used reason to understand human nature and society

c. a thinker who seeks wisdom

d. the rights people are born with, including the rights to life, liberty, and property

e. freedom

f. a system of government in which all citizens share in running the government

g. free of being ruled by another country

h. having the same rights as other people

i. having fair laws

j. to make sure

rationalism	philosopher	liberty	independent	justice
Enlightenment	natural rights	democracy	equality	guarantee

B. *Choose and write the two words that best complete each sentence.*

liberty	independent	democracy	guarantee

1. American colonists wanted to be _____ of British rule and

   form a new government that would _____ their rights.

justice	rationalism	natural rights	Enlightenment

2. Thinkers living during the _____ used

   _____ to understand the world, just as ancient Greek and

   Roman thinkers had.

natural rights	equality	philosopher	independent

3. John Locke, an English _____ , believed that people had

   _____ , such as life, liberty, and property.

rationalism	democracy	Enlightenment	liberty

4. Freedom, or _____ , was very important to Americans as

   they formed their new _____ .

equality	philosopher	guarantee	justice

5. Thomas Jefferson used ideas about liberty, _____ , and

   _____ when writing the Declaration of Independence.

WORD ROOT

The word **philosopher** comes from the Greek
words **philos**, which means "loving," and
sophos, which means "wisdom."

rationalism	philosopher	liberty	independent	justice
Enlightenment	natural rights	democracy	equality	guarantee

C. *Choose the correct vocabulary word to complete each sentence.*

1. The right of freedom is called _____ .

2. American colonists wanted to form a _____ , in which all citizens would share in running the government.

3. Americans wanted their government to _____ their rights to liberty, equality, and justice.

4. The French _____ Rousseau believed that citizens should share in running the government.

5. The roots of the Enlightenment go back to classical times, when ancient Greek and Roman thinkers used _____ to understand the world.

6. In the Declaration of Independence, Jefferson included ideas about _____ , or having fair laws.

7. American colonial leaders wanted the colonies to become _____ from Great Britain.

8. The ideas of the _____ led to changes in society and government.

9. Life, liberty, and property are all examples of _____ .

10. All Americans have the same rights, or _____ , under the law.

The Enlightenment

rationalism   philosopher   liberty   independent   justice
Enlightenment   natural rights   democracy   equality   guarantee

D. *Use each word in a sentence that shows you understand the meaning of the word.*

1. rationalism _____
   _____

2. natural rights _____
   _____

3. liberty _____
   _____

4. equality _____
   _____

5. justice _____
   _____

6. Enlightenment _____
   _____

7. guarantee _____
   _____

8. philosopher _____
   _____

9. democracy _____
   _____

10. independent _____
    _____

Write!

*Write your response to the prompt on a separate sheet of paper.
Use as many vocabulary words as you can in your writing.*

Imagine you are either Benjamin Franklin or Thomas Jefferson, visiting
Europe and learning about Enlightenment ideas. Write a letter home to a
friend, explaining what these new ideas might mean to the American colonies.

My Social Studies Vocabulary

Lesson 1: The Fall of the Roman Empire

_____   _____   _____

_____   _____   _____

_____   _____   _____

_____   _____   _____

_____   _____   _____

Lesson 2: The Byzantine Empire

_____   _____   _____

_____   _____   _____

_____   _____   _____

_____   _____   _____

_____   _____   _____

Lesson 3: The Muslim Empire

_____   _____   _____

_____   _____   _____

_____   _____   _____

_____   _____   _____

_____   _____   _____

Lesson 4: China in the Middle Ages

_____   _____   _____

_____   _____   _____

_____   _____   _____

_____   _____   _____

_____   _____   _____

Lesson 5: Empires of West Africa

_____   _____   _____

_____   _____   _____

_____   _____   _____

_____   _____   _____

_____   _____   _____

Lesson 6: Japan in the Middle Ages

_____   _____   _____

_____   _____   _____

_____   _____   _____

_____   _____   _____

My Social Studies Vocabulary

Lesson 7: Medieval Europe

_____   _____   _____

_____   _____   _____

_____   _____   _____

_____   _____   _____

_____   _____   _____

Lesson 8: The Role of the Church in Medieval Europe

_____   _____   _____

_____   _____   _____

_____   _____   _____

_____   _____   _____

_____   _____   _____

Lesson 9: Early Civilizations of the Americas

_____   _____   _____

_____   _____   _____

_____   _____   _____

_____   _____   _____

_____   _____   _____

Lesson 10: The Renaissance

_____   _____   _____

_____   _____   _____

_____   _____   _____

_____   _____   _____

_____   _____   _____

Lesson 11: Leading Figures and Achievements of the Renaissance

_____   _____   _____

_____   _____   _____

_____   _____   _____

_____   _____   _____

_____   _____   _____

Lesson 12: The Reformation

_____   _____   _____

_____   _____   _____

_____   _____   _____

_____   _____   _____

_____   _____   _____

My Social Studies Vocabulary

Lesson 13: The Scientific Revolution

_____   _____   _____

_____   _____   _____

_____   _____   _____

_____   _____   _____

_____   _____   _____

Lesson 14: The Age of Exploration

_____   _____   _____

_____   _____   _____

_____   _____   _____

_____   _____   _____

_____   _____   _____

Lesson 15: The Enlightenment

_____   _____   _____

_____   _____   _____

_____   _____   _____

_____   _____   _____

My Social Studies Vocabulary

Root Words

A word that is the beginning, or source, of a new word is called a "root word." Many English words have roots in other languages. Latin and Greek are two languages that have given English many new words. The study of history is rich in words that come to English from these languages. The word *history* itself comes from a Latin word *historia*, which means "story" or "tale."

This chart shows some Greek and Latin roots, their meanings, and examples of English words that use the roots. Use the space provided to write other words with the same roots and to add new roots, meanings, and examples.

Latin or Greek Root	Meaning	Examples
terra	land	territory, _____ , _____ , _____
schola	school	scholar, _____ , _____ , _____
astro	star	astrolabe, _____ , _____ , _____
urb	city	urban, _____ , _____ , _____
_____	_____	_____ , _____
_____	_____	_____ , _____
_____	_____	_____ , _____
_____	_____	_____ , _____

Prefixes and Suffixes

Prefixes

A prefix is a group of letters added to the beginning of a word to change the meaning. For example, *un-* is a prefix that means "not." Adding *un-* to *clear* makes the word *unclear*, which means "not clear." Add your own prefixes, meanings, and examples in the space below.

Prefix	Meaning	Examples
pro-	forward	proportion, _____ , _____
tele-	far	telescope, _____ , _____
micro-	small	microscope, _____ , _____
_____	_____	_____ , _____ , _____
_____	_____	_____ , _____ , _____

Suffixes

A suffix is a group of letters added to the end of a word to change the meaning. For example, *-er* is a suffix that means "one who." Adding *-er* to *teach* makes the word *teacher*, which means "one who teaches." Add your own suffixes, meanings, and examples in the spaces below.

Suffix	Meaning	Examples
-ism	system	feudalism, _____ , _____
-ship	state of, quality of	kinship, _____ , _____
-tion	action of	appreciation, _____ , _____
_____	_____	_____ , _____ , _____
_____	_____	_____ , _____ , _____

Glossary

Aa

adviser (ad-VY-zuhr)
a person who gives
advice
(Lesson 2, page 11)

agriculture
(AG-ruh-kuhl-chuhr)
farming
(Lesson 9, page 52)

anatomy
(uh-NAT-uh-mee)
the study of the human
body
(Lesson 11, page 65)

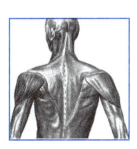

appreciation (uh-pree-shee-AY-shuhn)
understanding
(Lesson 10, page 59)

apprentice (uh-PREHN-tihs)
a beginner in an art or a trade
(Lesson 11, page 65)

archipelago
(ahr-kuh-PEHL-uh-goh)
a group or chain of islands
(Lesson 6, page 34)

architecture (AHR-kuh-tehk-chuhr)
the art of constructing buildings
(Lesson 9, page 53)

arid (AR-ihd)
dry; having very little rainfall
(Lesson 3, page 16)

artisan (AHR-tuh-zuhn)
a skilled craftsperson
(Lesson 4, page 23)

astrolabe (AS-truh-layb)
an instrument used
to find a ship's latitude
(Lesson 14, page 83)

astronomy
(uh-STRON-uh-mee)
the study of the stars and planets
(Lesson 11, page 65)

Bb

barter (BAHR-tuhr)
to trade goods without using money
(Lesson 1, page 5)

Buddhism
(BOO-dihz-uhm)
the religion that began in
India and is based on the
teachings of Buddha
(Lesson 4, page 22)

bureaucracy (byu-ROK-ruh-see)
a system of departments that carry out the
work of a government
(Lesson 4, page 23)

Cc

caliph (KAY-lihf)
a Muslim ruler
(Lesson 3, page 17)

capital (KAP-uh-tuhl)
the center of a country's government
(Lesson 1, page 4)

capitalism (KAP-uh-tuhl-lihz-uhm)
an economic system in which private owners control and use resources for profit
(Lesson 14, page 83)

caravan (KAR-uh-van)
a group of people traveling together by camel
(Lesson 3, page 16)

caravel (KAR-uh-vehl)
a ship with special sails designed for long voyages
(Lesson 14, page 83)

cartographer (kahr-TOG-ruh-fuhr)
a mapmaker
(Lesson 14, page 83)

cathedral
(kuh-THEE-druhl)
a large, important church
(Lesson 8, page 47)

chivalry (SHIHV-uhl-ree)
a code of behavior by which knights were expected to be brave, loyal, and kind
(Lesson 7, page 40)

Christianity (krihs-chee-AN-uh-tee)
a religion based on the life and teachings of Jesus
(Lesson 2, page 11)

clan (klan)
a kinship group related to a common ancestor
(Lesson 5, page 29)

classics (KLAS-ihks)
the works of ancient Greek and Roman writers
(Lesson 10, page 58)

clergy (KLUR-jee)
religious officials
(Lesson 8, page 46)

code (kohd)
a group of laws organized in a clear way
(Lesson 2, page 11)

colony (KOL-uh-nee)
a place that is controlled by another country
(Lesson 14, page 83)

Columbian Exchange
(kuh-LUHM-bee-uhn ehks-CHAYNJ)
the movement of people, plants, animals, and diseases between the Eastern and Western hemispheres
(Lesson 14, page 83)

commerce (KOM-uhrs)
the buying and selling of goods in large amounts over long distances
(Lesson 14, page 83)

commission (kuh-MIHSH-uhn)

an order for a work of art to be created
(*Lesson 11, page 65*)

conquer (KONG-kuhr)

to defeat
(*Lesson 1, page 5*)

conquistador

(kon-KEES-tuh-dawr)
a Spanish explorer and
soldier who conquered
native people in the
Americas
(*Lesson 9, page 53*)

constitution (kon-stuh-TOO-shuhn)

a written plan of government
(*Lesson 6, page 34*)

corrupt (kuh-RUHPT)

dishonest
(*Lesson 1, page 5*)

crossroads (KRAWS-rohdz)

a place where roads come together
(*Lesson 5, page 29*)

crusade (kroo-SAYD)

a Christian military
expedition to
Jerusalem in the
Middle Ages
(*Lesson 8, page 47*)

culture (KUHL-chuhr)

the way of life of a group of people
(*Lesson 5, page 28*)

Dd

daimyo (DY-myoh)

Japanese lords with large estates
(*Lesson 6, page 35*)

decline (dih-KLYN)

to grow weak
(*Lesson 1, page 5*)

decree (dih-KREE)

an order given by a ruler
(*Lesson 8, page 47*)

democracy (dih-MOK-ruh-see)

a system of government in which all citizens
share in running the government
(*Lesson 15, page 89*)

dynasty (DY-nuh-steh)

a series of rulers from the same family
(*Lesson 4, page 22*)

Ee

emperor (EHM-puhr-uhr)

the male ruler of an empire
(*Lesson 1, page 4*)

empire (EHM-pyr)

a large area of land ruled by one person
(*Lesson 1, page 4*)

Enlightenment (ehn-LY-tuhn-muhnt)
a period in which European thinkers used reason to understand human nature and society
(*Lesson 15, page 88*)

equality (ih-KWOL-uh-tee)
the state of having the same rights as other people
(*Lesson 15, page 89*)

Ff

faith (fayth)
belief in God
(*Lesson 12, page 70*)

feudalism (FYOO-duh-lihz-uhm)
a system of government that developed in the Middle Ages in Europe
(*Lesson 7, page 40*)

foundation (fown-DAY-shuhn)
a base for something
(*Lesson 2, page 10*)

Gg

geography (jee-OG-ruh-fee)
the physical features of a region
(*Lesson 5, page 28*)

gravity (GRAV-uh-tee)
the force that causes objects to have weight and move toward each other
(*Lesson 13, page 77*)

griot (gree-OH)
a storyteller
(*Lesson 5, page 29*)

guarantee (gar-uhn-TEE)
to make sure
(*Lesson 15, page 89*)

guild (gihld)
a group formed in Medieval Europe by people with the same trade or craft
(*Lesson 7, page 41*)

Hh

haiku (HY-koo)
a short poem arranged in three lines
(*Lesson 6, page 35*)

heliocentric (hee-lee-oh-SEHN-trihk)
sun-centered
(*Lesson 13, page 76*)

heretic (HEHR-uh-tihk)
a person who holds a belief that is different from what is accepted
(*Lesson 12, page 71*)

humanism (HYOO-muh-nihz-uhm)
a way of thought that focuses on human interests and achievements
(*Lesson 10, page 58*)

hypothesis (hy-POTH-uh-sihs)
an unproved explanation of facts
(*Lesson 13, page 77*)

Ii

imperial (ihm-PIHR-ee-uhl)
relating to an empire or emperor
(Lesson 4, page 23)

independent (ihn-dih-PEHN-duhnt)
free of being ruled by another country
(Lesson 15, page 89)

indulgence
(ihn-DUHL-juhns)
a pardon for a person's
sins
(Lesson 12, page 70)

Inquisition (ihn-kwuh-ZIHSH-uhn)
a court established by the Catholic Church
to investigate people accused of non-
Catholic beliefs
(Lesson 12, page 71)

interpret (ihn-TUR-priht)
to explain the meaning of
(Lesson 12, page 71)

Islam (IHS-luhm)
the religion based on the teachings of
Muhammad
(Lesson 3, page 17)

isolated (Y-suh-lay-tuhd)
separated
(Lesson 6, page 34)

Jj

justice (JUHS-tihs)
the state of having fair laws
(Lesson 15, page 89)

Kk

kabuki (kah-BOO-kee)
a form of Japanese drama that combines
singing, dancing, bold makeup, and
elaborate costumes
(Lesson 6, page 35)

kinship (KIHN-shihp)
a family relationship
(Lesson 5, page 29)

knight (nyt)
an armored warrior
who fought on
horseback
(Lesson 7, page 40)

Ll

latitude (LAT-uh-tood)
the distance north or south of the equator
(Lesson 14, page 83)

legend (LEHJ-uhnd)
a story about the past
(Lesson 9, page 53)

liberty (LIHB-uhr-tee)
freedom
(Lesson 15, page 89)

literature (LIHT-uhr-uh-chur)
written works
(Lesson 11, page 65)

Mm

Magna Carta (MAG-nuh KAHR-tuh)
a list of political rights written by England's nobles and signed by King John
(Lesson 7, page 41)

maize (mayz)
a type of corn
(Lesson 9, page 52)

manor (MAN-uhr)
a lord's estate
(Lesson 7, page 41)

maritime (MAR-uh-tym)
relating to the sea
(Lesson 4, page 23)

masterpiece
(MAS-tuhr-pees)
an outstanding work of art
(Lesson 10, page 59)

medieval (mee-dee-EE-vuhl)
having to do with the Middle Ages
(Lesson 7, page 40)

merchant (MUR-chuhnt)
a person who makes money by buying and selling goods
(Lesson 2, page 10)

Mesoamerica (mez-oh-uh-MEHR-uh-kuh)
the region that includes Mexico and Central America; Middle America
(Lesson 9, page 52)

microscope
(MY-kruh-skohp)
an instrument that makes very small things look bigger
(Lesson 13, page 77)

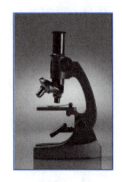

monastery (MON-uh-stehr-ee)
a place where monks lived quiet lives of prayer and worship
(Lesson 8, page 46)

mosaic (moh-ZAY-ihk)
a picture made from small pieces of colored stone or glass
(Lesson 2, page 11)

Muslim (MUHZ-luhm)
a person who believes in Islam
(Lesson 3, page 17)

Glossary

Nn

natural resources
(NACH-uhr-uhl rih-SOHR-sihz)
materials found in nature
(*Lesson 5, page 28*)

natural rights (NACH-uhr-uhl ryts)
the rights people are born with, including
the rights to life, liberty, and property
(*Lesson 15, page 89*)

navigator (NAV-uh-gay-tuhr)
a person who directs the route of a ship
(*Lesson 14, page 82*)

nomad (NOH-mad)
a person who moves from place to place,
usually in search of food and water
(*Lesson 3, page 16*)

Oo

oasis (oh-AY-sihs)
an area in the desert that has water from
underground
(*Lesson 3, page 16*)

orbit (AWR-biht)
the path of one object around another
in space
(*Lesson 13, page 76*)

Pp

parliament (PAHR-luh-muhnt)
a governing body made up of a group of
representatives
(*Lesson 7, page 41*)

patron (PAY-truhn)
a person who helps an artist or writer by
giving money
(*Lesson 10, page 59*)

perspective (puhr-SPEHK-tihv)
a technique in art that makes objects
on a flat surface appear to have distance
and depth
(*Lesson 11, page 64*)

philosopher
(fuh-LOS-uh-fuhr)
a thinker who seeks wisdom
(*Lesson 15, page 88*)

pilgrim (PIHL-gruhm)
a religious person who
travels to
a holy place
(*Lesson 8, page 47*)

pilgrimage (PIHL-gruh-mihj)
a journey to a holy place
(*Lesson 3, page 17*)

playwright (PLAY-ryt)
a person who writes
plays
(*Lesson 11, page 65*)

pope (pohp)
the leader of the Roman Catholic Church
(Lesson 8, page 46)

porcelain (POHR-suh-lihn)
a hard, white pottery made from fine clay
(Lesson 4, page 23)

portrait (POHR-triht)
a painting or drawing of a person
(Lesson 11, page 65)

preach (preech)
to teach a religious message
(Lesson 3, page 17)

priest (preest)
a member of the Catholic clergy who performed religious ceremonies
(Lesson 8, page 46)

printing press
(PRIHN-tihng prehs)
a machine that pressed paper against inked, movable type
(Lesson 10, page 59)

prophet (PROF-iht)
a person who is inspired to speak for God
(Lesson 3, page 17)

proportion (pruh-POHR-shuhn)
a technique in art that shows the relationship between objects in terms of size and shape
(Lesson 11, page 64)

prosperous (PROS-puhr-uhs)
rich
(Lesson 5, page 29)

protest (PROH-tehst)
an expression of disagreement
(Lesson 12, page 70)

Protestant
(PROT-uh-stuhnt)
a Christian who broke away from the Catholic Church
(Lesson 12, page 71)

public (PUHB-lihk)
known to all
(Lesson 12, page 70)

Qq

quipu (KEE-poo)
an Inca counting tool made of knotted strings
(Lesson 9, page 53)

Rr

rank (rangk)
social class
(Lesson 4, page 23)

rationalism (RASH-uh-nuh-lihz-uhm)
the use of reason to understand the world
(Lesson 15, page 88)

reform (rih-FAWRM)
to improve
(Lesson 2, page 11)

Reformation (rehf-uhr-MAY-shuhn)
a religious movement against the
Catholic Church
(Lesson 12, page 71)

Renaissance (REHN-uh-sahns)
a period of renewed creativity and great
achievements in the arts in Europe
(Lesson 10, page 58)

reunite (ree-yoo-NYT)
to bring together again
(Lesson 4, page 22)

revenue (REHV-uh-noo)
money that a government receives
(Lesson 5, page 29)

revolution (rehv-uh-LOO-shuhn)
a major change
(Lesson 13, page 76)

Ss _____

sacred (SAY-krihd)
holy
(Lesson 8, page 47)

sacrifice (SAK-ruh-fys)
the killing of animals or humans to please
the gods
(Lesson 9, page 52)

saint (saynt)
a holy person
(Lesson 2, page 11)

samurai (SAM-u-ry)
a highly skilled Japanese warrior
(Lesson 6, page 35)

savanna (suh-VAN-uh)
a grassy plain with
few trees
(Lesson 5, page 28)

scholar (SKOL-uhr)
a learned person
(Lesson 2, page 11)

scholar-official (SKOL-uhr-uh-FIHSH-uhl)
a learned person in China with a
government job
(Lesson 4, page 23)

scientific method
(sy-uhn-TIHF-ihk MEHTH-uhd)
an organized approach to scientific
investigation
(Lesson 13, page 77)

secular (SEHK-yuh-uhr)
related to things that are not religious
(Lesson 10, page 58)

seminary (SEHM-uh-nehr-ee)
a school for training priests
(Lesson 12, page 71)

senate (SEHN-iht)
a body of the
government that
makes laws
(Lesson 1, page 5)

serf (surf)
a peasant farmer in Medieval Europe who was tied to the land
(Lesson 7, page 41)

Shinto (SHIHN-toh)
a traditional Japanese religion based on respect for nature and ancestors
(Lesson 6, page 34)

shogun (SHOH-guhn)
a military leader who ruled Japan
(Lesson 6, page 35)

sponsor (SPON-suhr)
a person who gives money to support a project
(Lesson 14, page 82)

Tt

tax (taks)
the money people pay to support the government
(Lesson 1, page 5)

technique (tehk-NEEK)
a method used to make something
(Lesson 11, page 64)

telescope
(TEHL-uh-skohp)
an instrument that makes things that are far away look bigger
(Lesson 13, page 77)

terrain (teh-RAYN)
landscape
(Lesson 9, page 53)

territory (TEHR-uh-tawr-ee)
a large area of land
(Lesson 1, page 4)

theory (THEE-uhr-ee)
an explanation of how or why something happens
(Lesson 13, page 76)

thermometer
(thuhr-MOM-uh-tuhr)
an instrument that measures how hot or cold something is
(Lesson 13, page 77)

trade (trayd)
the buying and selling of goods
(Lesson 2, page 10)

tribute (TRIHB-yoot)
a forced payment in goods from a conquered people to a ruler
(Lesson 9, page 53)

Glossary

Uu

university
(yoo-nuh-VUR-suh-tee)
a school of advanced learning
(Lesson 8, page 47)

urban (UR-buhn)
relating to a city
(Lesson 10, page 59)

Vv

vassal (VAS-uhl)
a person who received land and protection
from a lord in return for loyalty
(Lesson 7, page 40)

vernacular (vuhr-NAK-yuh-luhr)
a person's native language
(Lesson 10, page 59)

Zz

Zen (zehn)
a form of Japanese Buddhism that focuses
on achieving inner peace
(Lesson 6, page 35)

Acknowledgments

Developer: Maureen Devine Sotoohi
Writer: Lisa Torrey
Cover Design: Susan Hawk
Designer: Pat Lucas
Photo Credits:

Cover: clockwise from top left: © 2007 JupiterImages Corporation; Reunion des Musees Nationaux/Art Resource, NY; © Bettmann/CORBIS; Daniel Loncarevic/Shutterstock.com

p. 5   (top) © 2007 JupiterImages Corporation; (bottom) © Baldwin H. Ward & Kathryn C. Ward/CORBIS

p. 10   Scala/Art Resource, NY

p. 11   (top, middle, bottom) © 2007 JupiterImages Corporation

p. 16   Vova Pomortzeff/Shutterstock.com

p. 22   (top) Moiss/Shutterstock.com; (bottom) Snark/Art Resource, NY

p. 23   (top) Reunion des Musees Nationaux/Art Resource, NY; (bottom) © Royal Ontario Museum/CORBIS

p. 28   Eric Isselee/Shutterstock.com

p. 29   Werner Forman/Art Resource, NY

p. 34   © 2007 JupiterImages Corporation

p. 35   (top) Library of Congress, Prints & Photographs Division, LC-USZC4-8655; (bottom) © Pierre Perrin/Sygma/Corbis

p. 40   Erich Lessing/Art Resource, NY

p. 41   (left) © Bettmann/CORBIS; (right) © Bettmann/CORBIS

p. 46   Giraudon/Art Resource, NY

p. 47   © 2007 JupiterImages Corporation

p. 52   HIP/Art Resource, NY

p. 53   (top) Daniel Loncarevic/Shutterstock.com; (bottom) © Gianni Dagli Orti/CORBIS

p. 59   (top) Vanni/Art Resource, NY; (Bottom) Erich Lessing/Art Resource, NY

p. 64   Scala/Art Resource, NY

p. 65   © 2007 JupiterImages Corporation

p. 70   The Pierpont Morgan Library/Art Resource, NY

p. 71   (left) Foto Marburg/Art Resource, NY; (right) © 2007 JupiterImages Corporation

p. 77   © 2007 JupiterImages Corporation

p. 83   (left) © 2007 JupiterImages Corporation

p. 88   © 2007 JupiterImages Corporation

p. 89   (left) Library of Congress, Famous People: Selected Portraits from the Collection of the Library of Congress, LC-USZ62-59655; (right) Library of Congress, Prints & Photographs Division, LC-H8-CT-C01-063-E

p. 101   (adviser) Scala/Art Resource, NY; (anatomy) © 2007 JupiterImages Corporation; (astrolabe) © 2007 JupiterImages Corporation; (Buddhism) Moiss/Shutterstock.com

p. 102   (caravel) © 2007 JupiterImages Corporation; (cathedral) Alexander Shargin/Shutterstock.com

p. 103   (conquistador) © 2007 JupiterImages Corporation; (crusade) © 2007 JupiterImages Corporation; (emperor) © 2007 JupiterImages Corporation

p. 105   (indulgence) © Bettmann/CORBIS; (knight) © 2007 JupiterImages Corporation

p. 106   (maize) © 2007 JupiterImages Corporation; (masterpiece) © 2007 JupiterImages Corporation; (microscope) Milos Luzanin/Shutterstock.com; (mosaic) Scala/Art Resource, NY

p. 107   (oasis) POZZO DI BORGO Thomas; (philosopher) © 2007 JupiterImages Corporation; (playwright) © 2007 JupiterImages Corporation

p. 108   (printing press) © 2007 JupiterImages Corporation; (quipu) © Gianni Dagli Orti/CORBIS

p. 109   (saint) © 2007 JupiterImages Corporation; (savanna) Eric Isselée/Shutterstock.com; (senate) © Baldwin H. Ward & Kathryn C. Ward/CORBIS

p. 110   (thermometer) © 2007 JupiterImages Corporation

p. 111   (urban) Vianni/Art Resource, NY

Illustration Credits:

pp. 4, 17, (top) 29, (top) 34, 58, 76, 82, (right) 83, 101 Pat Lucas